MW00992713

Fear & Anger

Slay the Dragons That Hold You Back!

Written by Lynette Hanthorn
Edited by National Press Publications

NATIONAL PRESS PUBLICATIONS

A Division of Rockhurst College Continuing Education Center, Inc.

6901 West 63rd Street • P.O. Box 2949 • Shawnee Mission, Kansas 66201-1349

1-800-258-7248 • 1-913-432-7757

National Press Publications endorses non-sexist language. In an effort to make this handbook clear, consistent and easy to read, we've used "he" throughout the odd-numbered chapters and "she" throughout the even-numbered chapters. The copy is not intended to be sexist.

Fear & Anger — Slay the Dragons That Hold You Back!
Copyright 1996, National Press Publications, Inc.
Published by National Press Publications, Inc.
A Division of Rockhurst College Continuing Education Center, Inc.

Printed in the United States of America

4 5 6 7 8 9 10

ISBN 1-55852-170-4

TABLE OF CONTENTS

1 LOOKING AT YOUR DRAGONS OF FEAR AND ANGER

Once upon a time — very early this morning, as a matter of fact — thousands of people across the land woke up and felt a deep sense of dread. You see, they lived in a land where terrible monsters — dragons actually — lay in wait to trap and devour them. These dragons were very cunning and the people were afraid of them. But nobody wanted to deal with the dragons, so everybody tried to pretend they didn't exist. But the dragons moved into the hearts of the people. Because they weren't supposed to tell anyone about the dragons living in their hearts, the people tried to ignore them even there. That left the dragons to merrily munch away at the people with whom they lived. So everyone lived with their dragons, not knowing that everyone else had a dragon too. They also didn't know that the clue for slaying the dragons was right before them. You see, the dragons all had one mother — and her name was Fear. Anger was her favorite son.

Fear Is the Motivator

Do you have some dragons in your life? Look around you. People are filing grievances and lawsuits, installing locks and security systems. More and more, we seem to be obsessed with protecting ourselves from the dragons breathing fire at our doors. We want to be sure that the dragons won't get us.

If unchecked, the dragon of fear can be a major motivator in your life. And no wonder! It has plenty to feed on in today's society! Every time you read a newspaper or watch the evening news on television, you learn about terrible crimes, dishonest national leaders, "scams" that destroy lives, and natural and man-made disasters. It's no wonder you feel you have to lock your doors at night!

Fear opens the gates to your darkest, most basic instincts for survival. You want to feel safe, so you do everything you can to protect yourself. You become suspicious of people who are different. You feel that your personal safety is threatened. You worry about things that "go bump" in the night. You resist the risks of charting the unknown fields of change.

The fears that you and those around you feel have a devastating effect in the workplace. Even if your fears are unjustified, you may worry about losing your job or your boss telling you that your performance is not up to par. You may fear that you are making the wrong career choices and will find out too late that you've been traveling on a dead-end street. Maybe you fear that you won't be taken seriously — that you present the "wrong" image. Or that the people who make the decisions for your company can't be trusted. You may even fear that you can't keep up with technology and that it's only a matter of time before some younger, brighter person will take your place.

Whatever you fear, one thing is certain — you're not alone. The people with whom you work, all of the significant people in your life, even the people you look up to and try to model your life after — they all experience fear in some form.

At its most basic level, fear is the feeling that you are not safe and that you are separated from others. Fear is a feeling of apprehension or dread of some perceived threat. Fear is the opposite of joy.

Fear is a very real emotion. It causes real physical and emotional sensations. Fear is the root of that sick feeling you get in your stomach when the boss, in an angry mood, tells you to get in his office, NOW! Fear is the nagging voice in your head that whispers that you're probably going to lose your job because you dropped the ball on your latest project. Fear causes your sleepless nights when you hear rumors that the company you work for is having financial problems.

Since there are so many things to be afraid of in today's world, it's only logical that you feel fearful, right?

Is it? Is it truly logical to feel fearful? Are all of *your* fears justified?

Let's look at the facts. According to psychologists, about 10 percent of your fears are based on real, tangible dangers to your being. This 10 percent includes things like the rush of fear you feel if you see a child step in front of an oncoming car, or the fear you would feel if you woke up in the middle of the night and saw a stranger standing over you.

The fear that you would feel is logical in these situations because of the very real possibility that you or someone else is in danger. It's at times like these that fear serves its best and highest purpose — to protect you from physical or emotional danger. Fear can make you more alert and focused on the problem. Fear can push you to take action to prevent the danger from harming you or others.

But what about the remaining 90 percent of your fears? They feel very real too. What are they based on?

These are the fears that are based on perceived or imagined dangers. They have no basis in reality. They are the fears you generate within yourself, and they can take as many forms as there are people with vivid imaginations.

For example, imagine that you had surgery and were required to take a great deal of sick leave from work. Further imagine that you have been wanting a promotion and have been working hard on a tricky project before the surgery. While you were gone, would you be concerned about what your boss was thinking about you? Would you be afraid that one of your co-workers might be doing your job better than you ever did? Would you be afraid that your job might be in jeopardy — even though your boss and co-workers expressed a great deal of sympathy and concern for your welfare?

Most people would feel a veritable cornucopia of fears in this situation. Do these fears feel real? Very much so. Do they have a basis in reality? Not really. Your boss and co-workers have expressed only concern for your recovery. The co-worker who is filling in for you calls regularly and gives you progress reports. You're being kept in the loop through copies of memos, and your boss assures you that as soon as you return to work, you and he will talk about your promotion.

So, how did you determine that there was something to fear in this situation? Easy. You generated your fear all by yourself. Insecurities, past guilts, a sense of shame over being ill — all of these things can lead your thinking to become fear-based. And since you tend to exaggerate the negative when your thinking is fear-based, you anticipate that the worst will happen.

This type of fear is especially destructive because it has a tendency to grow. You start with the imagined fear that your boss is angry with you for being gone from the office, and then a little voice says that he might fire you. Then you start worrying that your friend who is doing your work may not really be your friend at all, that maybe he is using this time to make you look bad, and on and on and on until you finally convince yourself that you have a roomful of fears to worry about.

The Fear of Talking About Fear

But who do you talk with about these fears? Often, the thought of talking about your fears spawns a whole new field of fears, such as "What if they laugh at me because I'm afraid?" or "What if he gets mad at me if I tell him I feel fearful when he does that?" or "What if they make me do something I'm not ready to do?" Or you think, "I'm afraid to have this person know my intimate fears." Or "What if he won't like me because I'm so weak and fearful?"

Indeed, the idea of talking about fear strikes at the five most common fears of people — the fear of conflict, the fear of commitment, the fear of intimacy, the fear of rejection and the fear of speaking up. Of these, the No. 1 fear is the fear of speaking up. For example, are you afraid that if you talk directly about disagreements in the workplace, there might be repercussions? Many people are afraid to speak up about the things that are bothering them. The problem with this line of thinking, however, is that when people don't communicate, their different points of view become major barriers to productive work performance. And often, the fear of speaking up leads to negative habits — such as withholding information that is needed to do a job, criticizing absent co-workers, feeling unsure about your ability to do the work, or giving up a cherished ambition.

To see how destructive the fear of speaking up can be, let's look at Randy, a welder, who worked the night shift at a local manufacturing plant. He took great pride in his work and consistently exceeded his quotas. He was happiest, however, when he was creating wonderful works of metal art in his garage workshop. He spent every afternoon there before coming to work. The art he produced was so beautiful that people came from miles around to buy pieces for their homes. In addition to augmenting his income, this side work also allowed him to tap into his innate creativity and to talk with many different people — things he loved to do but which were not encouraged in his job at the plant. Therefore, his creative work made him a better employee. He came to work refreshed. The needs he had that were not being met on the job were being satisfied.

5

As his side business grew, Randy bought a new truck and took his wife on a trip to the Bahamas. Jealous co-workers then started the rumor that Randy was stealing materials from the shop to create his art at home. They also hinted that he probably worked on his metal art during company time. One day, some employees ribbed the manager about Randy driving a newer vehicle than he was driving and suggested that maybe he ought to start "taking the company for a ride" as they suspected Randy was.

Randy was still doing an outstanding job, but his manager became suspicious. Although he never accused Randy of any wrongdoing, he wanted to keep his eye on him. So he asked Randy to start working the day shift.

Randy didn't want to work days, but he was afraid to tell his manager how important his side business was to him. Further, he was afraid if he said "no" to working days, he would lose his job. Reluctantly, he shut down his shop in the garage and complied with his manager's wishes.

But he became bitter and did as little as possible. He felt the company didn't care about him or how good a job he did. He decided that all the company wanted was to "squeeze the last ounce of blood out of him." His manager, on the other hand, read Randy's sullen mood and lackadaisical performance as confirmation that Randy had been doing something wrong. He reasoned that Randy's previous exemplary performance had only been a cover-up for his theft of time and materials. However, no one discussed the situation.

Randy's fear blocked communication and led to counterproductive actions. As Randy stopped performing as he had been, the unit's overall productivity and quality declined, leading his manager to develop his own fears about losing his job.

In Randy's case, as often happens, fear also wasted potential. Randy's fear of losing his job kept him from pursuing a hobby that might have become a rewarding new career. His fear prevented him from taking risks that would help him achieve his dreams.

Fear doesn't restrict you just once. It slows your growth by reliving negative experiences over and over, keeping you locked in a continuing cycle of failure. This cycle breeds yet more fears — enormous fears arising from feelings of inadequacy, a lack of personal power and a fear of loneliness. That's why it's so important in the workplace to manage not only your own fear but also the fear of the people around you. Unexplored emotions can be damaging. Negative emotions such as fear become dark very quickly and can overwhelm you and others, especially since they often lead to anger.

Anger often is the mask used to conceal fear and insecurity — a tool to protect yourself from actions that appear to be unjustified or intentional attacks on your activities, character and self-worth.

The Roots of Anger

When do you feel anger? Generally you feel angry when you are not getting what you want or need, or when you are blamed for something for which you are not responsible. For example, you may be angry when a co-worker leaves you with extra work because she takes a spur-of-the-moment vacation to the Bahamas, but you aren't angry about taking on extra work to help the same co-worker when she takes a leave of absence to care for a dying relative. Doing extra work in the second example makes you feel helpful, worthwhile and valued while in the first example you fear that no one respects or values you.

Along with anger often comes confusion. As a child, you were probably taught that it was wrong to get angry and that you were "bad" if you expressed your anger. Because of your early training, you may not be comfortable with either your own anger or the anger that others display. You may even try to avoid it at all costs.

The fact is, though, that anger is an inescapable reality of life. It must be addressed — not avoided. Anger is a message. By itself, it's neither good nor bad. In fact, anger can be healthy when you are attempting to resolve a conflict. Anger helps you focus on the issues that are important to you. Anger also makes you more aware of the differences you have with others and can strengthen your sense of why we need each other and what we have in common.

If you deny your anger or try to avoid it, you are avoiding a vital portion of yourself. Your anger is there for a reason. It's up to you to have the courage to look at it and understand what your anger is trying to tell you.

The Truth About Your Anger

When was the last time you felt angry? What made you angry? What did you feel was threatening you? Try thinking about your anger in the light of these six basic truths:

> *1. Anger is a message of what is happening within you.* It is easy to misread anger and allow yourself to feel rage, wrath, indignation, resentment, provocation or infuriation. When this happens, try to stop and ask yourself, "What is this about? What is making me furious?" Under the anger may be the fear that you are being taken advantage of, the fear that you always have to do this yourself, the fear that no one is there to take care of you, the fear of being betrayed, the fear of not being important.
>
> *2. Anger is not good or bad.* As a child, you may have been scolded for getting angry and learned that anger is a "bad" emotion. Further, you may have learned that you are bad if you are angry. But anger is not bad. Anger is simply the manifestation of the fear that you feel. It's what you do with your anger that can lead to positive (good) or negative (bad) results.

3. Anger can mean "I care." If you don't care about someone or something, you don't have any reason to get angry. Anger is an expression of your need for others. We all want to be cared about, listened to. We need to feel that our ideas are respected. We need to feel that our expectations for ourselves and others are understood. Anger says, "Let's look at my needs, your needs and our needs!"

4. Anger is misunderstood and mismanaged. If you have not learned how to deal with your anger, it is a very confusing emotion. Your parents and teachers probably taught you to avoid your anger, not manage it. In fact, most people are very skilled at *not* feeling or showing their anger. How then are you supposed to understand it in yourself or in others?

5. Anger can destroy communication and relationships. Unmanaged anger creates an atmosphere of distrust. It results in a sense of powerlessness, interferes with cooperation and increases fears of building relationships or confronting conflicts. Healthy, open and skillful expressions of anger, on the other hand, contribute to positive, open communication and establish good working relationships based on respect and understanding of needs.

6. Anger is part of being human. People who explode in anger are often viewed as immature and out of control. Yet everyone feels anger at times — and sometimes that is good. Anger gives you the power to make changes. Our history is filled with the accomplishments of angry people — people who used the strength of their anger to persevere against tremendous odds. When you misinterpret anger and try to deny it, you increase your fear and reduce your power. *Accepting your anger and learning to manage it is critical to fulfilling your potential as an intelligent, caring human being.*

"Safe" Ways to Handle Anger That Are Hazardous to Your Health

Because anger is such a dangerous emotion, most of us stick to *safe* ways to handle it. We try to keep it under control by dealing with it in one of the following ways:

You deny your anger by telling yourself that you really aren't angry — but you are. Especially when you feel you have a lot to lose — either in position or prestige — by showing your anger. You may think it's easier (at the moment) to say, *"I'm not angry. No, really. It's all right. I really don't feel angry."*

You repress your anger. This is a deeper form of denying your anger. You repress your anger, you push it deeply into your subconscious mind where it festers until, one day, it turns into rage. Repressed anger is the culprit behind innumerable emotional and physical ailments. It certainly is the root of hatred toward others. It can be recognized with statements like, *"Those incompetents! I* always *have to clean up their mess."*

You project your anger by pushing it off on someone else. If you can't feel angry yourself, you assume that the other person is feeling the anger that you are trying to deny. Let's say that you've just had a meeting with your boss, and he told you he's assigning a plum project to someone else. He gave you valid reasons for his decision — reasons that showed he had a lot of concern and respect for you. You were so angry, though, that you didn't really hear them. It was too risky to admit your anger, so all you heard in your head were the words, *"He's angry with me,"* as you projected your own feelings onto him.

You rationalize your anger by creating excuses for inappropriate or unacceptable behavior instead of getting angry. You decide that it is not worth the risk to show your anger, so you say things like, *"I'm not angry with her because she was trying so hard to do her best."* Or *"I'm not angry with him because that's just the way he is, and he's retiring soon anyway."*

If you're like most people, you probably handle anger in one or more of the above ways. There's a reason why you handle anger in these nonproductive ways: It is easier to deny/repress/project/rationalize your own emotions than to risk someone else reacting emotionally toward you.

However, you cannot control other people's emotions. You can only control your own and *the only way to manage anger is to be responsible for your whole self.*

Being responsible for your whole self means that you don't deny your anger or try to repress it. You take ownership of your anger rather than trying to give it away to someone else. You embrace your personal standards, rather than compromising them by making excuses for those who do not live up to them.

Only by understanding your anger can you discover what you care about. By accepting your anger, you focus your energies and become a powerful, caring, effective manager of people. You become a model from whom others can learn when you understand that fear and anger — in yourself and others — can make positive contributions to your relationships.

Your Anger Checklist

Part of understanding your anger is recognizing the fine line between using it and abusing it. Here is a checklist of questions to help you to determine which you do:

Do you use your anger to create a wall to help you feel safe? Anger is a good way to keep people at a distance. If you are always angry, people don't bother you with their concerns, and you don't have to deal with matters you feel you are not capable of handling.

Do you use your anger to demonstrate your power, pride, tenacity and commitment? Anger makes people take you seriously and gives you power to make other people do what you want — or at least wait to do what *they* want until they are out of your sight!

Do you use your anger to feel in control and strong? Anger can make you feel more sure of yourself. But anger that is summoned up merely for the sake of making you feel strong is misused anger. Do you feel that you need a *hit* of anger to perform effectively?

Do you use your anger to give you energy and a charge? Your anger stimulant can pump you up with a surge of energy, but like the need to feel angry to feel confident, anger for anger's sake can be an addictive part of your emotional make-up.

Do you use your anger to avoid revealing who you are? When you're always angry, no one stays around long enough to find out who you really are, and so you are *safe* from building relationships with others.

Do you use your anger to correct others and insist you are right? Anger can make others afraid to cross you and give you a sense of superiority that you may feel you lack.

Do you use your anger to punish others and make them feel guilty? When you direct your anger at others to punish them, it may make you feel more righteous. But most of all, anger used this way diverts attention from the pain you feel inside yourself at your own shortcomings.

Do you use your anger to avoid feelings of sadness, disappointment, loneliness, fear and abandonment? Anger gives you a feeling of *connectedness*. If you are busy feeling angry, you are justified in not feeling anything else.

Do you use your anger to keep you in the role of victim or persecutor? Anger can be a part of the self-fulfilling prophesy, chaining you to roles that you perceive as being successful for you.

Do you use your anger to hold on to relationships? When anger is the focus of your relationship, you not only avoid the vulnerability of exposing your true feelings, you also actively involve the other person — if only to defend himself or herself!

Do you use your anger to avoid taking responsibility for your actions? It's not easy to take responsibility for your actions, especially if those actions have had less than desirable consequences. Being angry means never having to say, "I'm sorry."

If you answered "yes" to any of these questions, ask yourself these questions:

What are you afraid of? Are you afraid that if you let someone see the *real* you, they won't like what they see? Have you even given them a chance?

What resentments are you hanging on to? Does your resentment serve any useful purpose in your life? Does it truly have any basis in reality?

What are you sad about? Wouldn't it be more healing to embrace the sadness and let yourself grieve so you can get on with your life?

What insecurities do you feel? Aren't there other ways that you can get the power, the control, the energy that you need — ways that won't drain your emotional self?

If it is too scary to deal with these questions by yourself, ask a trusted friend or mentor to assist you. We all need support as we work to understand our emotions.

You open doors to yourself and to others when you answer these questions. You learn to understand the true messages that your anger is trying to give you. It might seem scary, but only through understanding can you heal the wounds and go on to build the inner self that you want to be.

Feel the Fear

When you allow yourself to feel your fear and anger and then recognize their sources, you become stronger. You can respond from the strength of understanding, rather than react from the weaknesses of your fears. As you face your emotions and discover the real message behind them, you can see more clearly what you are doing and where you are going. You will be able to express your feelings more appropriately. Feel the fear, know it for what it is, recognize its cause — this is the key to understanding.

As a manager, your increased understanding of yourself will allow you to manage rather than react to the fear and anger of others. Although you are not responsible for the actions and thoughts of others, as a manager you may be held accountable for the negative consequences of those actions. Therefore, it is wise to follow steps that provide a deliberate approach to managing the negativity of others. That approach is the four Cs of problem-solving.

The Four Cs for Handling Problems

The first "C"

Clarify the issues. There is a difference between issues and events. *Issues* are problems or concerns. If you don't understand the issues in a problem, the issues turn into an event. An *event* occurs when you not only have the problems to contend with, but also have a flurry of emotions clouding the true meaning of the issues. Issues become events when you proceed to fix what you perceive is wrong before you bother finding out what the other person's problems are. Events occur most often because you don't want to endure the pain of an emotional encounter. You really don't want more information. When you turn issues into events, however, you destroy the learning process. In conflict, a certain level of frustration and pain is necessary for growth. The best way to keep issues from turning into events is to ask questions until you are sure you understand the issues, and then ask some more.

> Example:
>
> During a meeting with her manager, Barbara wants to express her fear abour losing her job. Her fear has become anger and now she's ready to *unload* on her boss. The conversation might go like this:
>
> Barbara: *"I'm sick and tired of always giving 110 percent for nothing, never getting decent benefits and not knowing if the company doors will stay open. I'm tired of being treated like a dog!"*
>
> **What does not work.** If the manager wants to avoid further discussion and stop this painful conversation as quickly as possible, she might say, *"I don't know what to tell you. Business is touch-and-go. Barbara, you're doing a great job."*

The manager has just sent a message that the business might fold and adds insult to injury by giving Barbara an empty compliment. The opportunity to clarify the issues has been missed.

What works. The manager determines that she needs to understand Barbara's feelings and what she is saying. She says, *"You sound really upset about an uncertain future and how you're being treated."*

Barbara fires back, *"I can't take this not knowing. You act as though you could care less when you say things like 'next month looks bad.' Maybe you don't care but I don't have any options if this place folds."*

The manager explores, *"Does it frighten you when you hear statements like that?"*

Throughout her conversation, the manager seeks to understand Barbara's concerns. Notice that she is not judgmental. She is careful to phrase her words so Barbara will feel safe to talk about her concerns.

The first step in solving any problem is to understand what the problem is. All too often, we try to jump in with a solution before we know what needs to be fixed. Take the time to clarify the issues, and you'll find that solutions will naturally follow.

The second "C"

Control the issues. If you don't control the direction of emotional conversations, you may find yourself dealing with the negative emotions of the involved parties and the residual waves caused by those emotions. You are not responsible for other people's emotions, and you should not attempt to control them, but as a manager, it is your responsibility to keep people focused on the problems they wish to address. You must keep the conversation focused on the concerns, needs, fears and goals of the emotional person.

> Example:
>
> After the manager asks if she correctly understands Barbara's concerns, Barbara responds, *"I need to feel good about being here, and I need to know what the future is for this place. And so does everyone else. Why can't you be straight with us for a change?"*
>
> **What does not work**. The manager may want to say, *"Hey, give me a break here. I'm on your side, remember?"* Barbara would probably then respond, *"On my side? You're not going to be on my side when I get laid off, and I know it. You don't care whether or not my kids get school clothes. You don't care about any of us. All you care about is making sure you're in good with management."* At this point, the conversation would quickly get derailed with the manager being put on the defensive and both parties engaging in a heated argument.
>
> **What works.** The manager says, *"It sounds to me like you're disappointed in how information has been handled here."* The manager keeps to the issues as Barbara brings them up, rephrasing them if necessary, but always searching for the problems that can be solved.

The third "C"

Confront the problem, not the person. When someone is being emotional, it's all too easy to focus on the person as the problem, rather than on the problem itself. Acknowledge the person but focus on what is really being expressed. When you're clear about the problem, then confront it. Don't wait, or you'll have to confront the person, and that's a great deal harder to do.

> Example:
>
> When the manager focuses on Barbara's disappointment, Barbara responds, *"I am disappointed. I used to respect you, but it's hard when I don't get treated with respect."*
>
> **What does not work**. If the manager says, *"What do you mean by that? I treat you with respect all the time. I'm giving you a job, aren't I?"* the conversation detours from problem-solving to defensiveness. The problem is forgotten while hard feelings grow.
>
> **What works.** The manager says, *"How do you see me not treating you with respect? What would make you feel more respected?"*
>
> Barbara responds, *"You can start by telling us what we need to know."*
>
> The manager focuses in and says, *"If I've understood, you feel I don't respect you when I don't give you enough information."*

The fourth "C"

Challenge the things that are said by the emotional person. When we feel angry or fearful, extremes are common and tunnel vision is likely. As a manager, you *must* keep the problem in perspective. You don't want to minimize or magnify the emotions and negative issues being expressed. You need to stay focused on the process of resolving the problem.

> Example:
>
> Barbara says, *"That's right. So is the rumor true? Are we closing?"*
>
> **What does not work.** The manager says, *"Hey, Barbara. A rumor's a rumor. Don't worry so much!"* Then Barbara responds, *"See, you never tell us what's going on."* The conversation gets side-tracked.
>
> **What does work.** The manager responds, *"I can tell you, at this time, the plant is not closing. The rumor is not true. But I know after our discussion that my comments are taken very seriously, and I need to be more careful about clarifying what I say. Do you have any other suggestions?"* The manager and Barbara continue talking.

By clarifying the issues, controlling the direction of the conversation, confronting the problem, not the person, and challenging the reality of the things that are being said, you will take giant strides toward managing the negativity of others. This approach will help you alleviate the fears people have and calm the anger they are feeling. Most of all, it draws the dragons of fear and anger out into the open. It provides a method for dealing with the dragons that empower you and those around you to build stronger, more healthy relationships.

Action Guidelines

1. Examine your fears.

2. Analyze your anger.

3. Find the *payoffs* of your fear and anger.

4. Decide to manage your fear and anger.

5. Determine the difference between issues and events in your life.

You don't have to be a victim of the "dragons." You turn off the "anxiety alarm" and take control of fear and anger when you do the following:

Clarify: How big is the dragon? Who is it bothering? What should not be ignored?

Control: Are you keeping your eye on the dragon?

Confront: Deal with the dragon, not the person.

Challenge: What's real about the dragon?

2 YOU ARE A WORTHY OPPONENT FOR YOUR DRAGON

So the brave citizen decided to look at her dragon, and it was a terrible thing to see. It blew smoke through its nose and had long, curved claws on its feet. The dragon looked very big indeed as it puffed itself up and roared, "How dare such a puny creature as you look upon me. Can't you see that I am mighty and you are nothing? Bow your head and submit to my will. Resign yourself to your fate, and accept that I will rule you forever." Just as the citizen was about to comply with the dragon's commands, she noticed something she had not seen before. She looked harder to see if her eyes were deceiving her. Could it be? Yes, through the darkness, she could see it! There was something dangling around the dragon's neck! It was a leash — a very strong leash attached to a wide silver collar! She ran into the dark cave and grabbed hold of the leash. "I'm not a puny creature," she declared. "Come out in the light, and let us do battle in the sun."

The Value of Self-Worth in Dealing with Fear and Anger

Do you feel that you are a worthy person? Do you feel that basically you are okay?

You know you have self-worth if you feel that you are a useful and valuable person. You feel you have something to contribute. You believe your thoughts and feelings deserve respect.

When you have a strong sense of self-worth, you are able to deal with fear and anger more positively because you can forgive yourself for having fears that are ungrounded. You don't have to resort to the ploys of anger to be taken seriously or gain power. Your power comes from the knowledge that you are all right. You don't have to pretend to be anyone other than who you are.

To be a healthy, happy person with self-worth, you need the approval of others and yourself. You need to like yourself and feel appreciated by those who are closest to you. You need affection and a sense of belonging. You need to feel that you are included.

You also need justice. You need to feel that there is equality, equity and fairness in your world. And you need a sense of power. You need to feel that you are able to influence others and make a real difference in the world around you. Lastly, you need your own identity. You need to have a positive self-image and feel that you have autonomy.

As a child and as an adult, you may not have had the opportunity to develop a good sense of your self-worth. There may not have been people in your life who sent you the message that you were all right just the way you were.

Instead, you may have been conditioned to believe that your value comes from outside of you, that your identity is based on what you do and have done in the past.

You may even feel like your mind is a recording device and a lot of people want to program it. Day in and day out, you hear the messages asking you, "What do you do? What have you achieved?"

You play these messages in your head again and again. You also play recordings of your past experiences, including those that made you feel fear and anger. Many times, these messages color how you feel. They may even blind you to what you really need. Let's say that as a child, you had a good reason to fear strangers. Your parents told you not to talk to strangers or accept anything from them. So you learned to fear strangers. But now that you're an adult, you sometimes have to talk to strangers to do your job. If the message your parents gave you keeps playing in your head, you're going to find it hard to do your job, aren't you?

Fortunately, there is an even greater fear that helps you overcome all others — the fear for survival. Going back to the example of being afraid of strangers, you may hear the message, but then the fear for survival kicks in saying, "But I'm no longer a child. I can judge whether or not I should speak to this stranger. And if I don't do my job, I'm not going to eat."

The fear for survival is a powerful impetus to grow beyond outdated messages, but something deep inside you may hold you back from reaching your full potential — something prevents you from truly breaking free of outgrown assumptions and inner messages. That something is shame.

Living with Shame

Shame is a close cousin of fear. The dictionary defines shame as a strong sense of guilt, embarrassment, unworthiness or disgrace. Shame is the opposite of self-worth.

Most people feel shame at some time in their lives. All too often, people who feel shame want to make other people feel shame too. It's the old *misery loves company* syndrome.

Shame often begins in childhood when your perceptions and beliefs are distorted by fear. For example, a neighborhood bully yells, "Get out of here, you little twerp! We don't need you." You feel you don't belong. You're ashamed because you think there is something wrong with you. You're embarrassed because you thought you *did* belong, but you were wrong.

Or maybe your mother said something like, "Why can't you be like your cousin Nancy? She's so pretty and ..." You felt unworthy, that you didn't measure up, that you were not okay just as you were.

A sense of shame undermines your self-worth by placing the mantle of *victim* on your shoulders and making you feel that you are not capable or worthy.

The Destruction of Trust

Worst of all, shame destroys trust. Shame causes you to ask yourself the questions, "Where do I belong?" and "What can I expect from the world?"

When you feel a deep sense of shame, you cannot trust yourself or anyone else. And what you cannot trust, you fear. From this, you develop the philosophy that trust is something that must be earned, usually through tests for yourself and others. When you or others cannot pass the tests, you feel justified in your fear of trusting them.

In reality, life works differently. You trust others to the degree that you trust yourself. And trust is to be given, not earned.

But even if you carry around a heavy burden of shame, you still must function in the world. Therefore, you learn to put on a false face, suppressing your true feelings. You bury your feelings deeper and deeper until you no longer recognize how much they influence everything you say and do. Because you no longer can identify your feelings, you never give yourself the opportunity to discover whether or not your feelings have a basis in the real world.

The Circle of Shame

If you have experienced tremendous shame in your life, you may feel anger. You may also have buried the anger about your shame deep inside yourself and feel guilt about your failed attempts to repair bonds and relationships. As this occurs again and again, you may become depressed. The depression makes you feel even more ashamed and unlovable. So if your anger is not expressed, you get caught up in a circle of shame that looks like this:

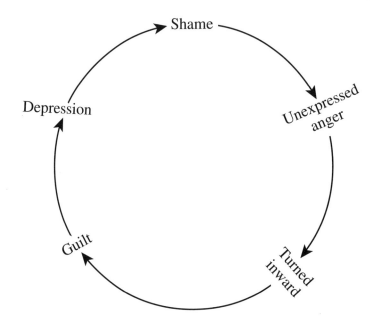

Breaking the Circle of Shame

Left unchecked, this circle of shame repeats itself over and over. You repeat the same situations over and over without realizing it. You try different roads, but they all turn out to be dead ends. The only way to break this circle of shame is to take steps to heal yourself and see the world in a new way.

The first step in breaking the circle of shame is to find a safe environment. Fear — the root of your shame — feeds on insecurity and danger. Create a space where you feel safe from the things that make you afraid and feel shame. Surround yourself with friends you can confide in, or find a professional counselor whom you trust. Get the resources you need to feel safe so you can work on breaking the circle of shame.

The second step is to recognize and release the anger you feel. Within your safe environment, express the feelings you have. Release the emotions that have always seemed too scary to talk about. Allow yourself to admit your anger.

The third step is to explore who you really are and identify where you are "stuck" emotionally. To aid this process, answer the following questions:

Who was the most influential person in your life?

How would you describe this person? Was she generally positive or negative? Did she encourage you or discourage you? Did you feel worthy when you were around her, or did you feel that you disappointed her?

How did you feel about this person? Did you like her? Were you afraid of her? Did you dread talking to her? Were you cautious about revealing your true feelings to her? Did you feel good when you were around her? Did she make you feel that you had personal power?

When was the first time you remember feeling shamed?

What do you remember seeing when you felt shamed?

What do you remember hearing when you felt shamed?

What else did you feel regarding that incident?

Once you have explored the roots of your shame, allow yourself to feel sorrow about the shame and then release it. Allow yourself to grieve over the incident that caused the shame.

With your shame behind you, you will be ready to grow and start perceiving things in a new light. Learn to identify and recognize your feelings as they happen. This will take some practice, and you certainly won't be able to monitor every feeling you have each day. But try to identify the significant ones — the ones that have the greatest impact on you. When you go to work and discover that a co-worker has borrowed your favorite pen — again — and forgotten to bring it back, identify the feeling you have. Give it a voice by saying to yourself: "I feel _____ when this happens." Once you become comfortable expressing your feelings to yourself, start expressing those same feelings to others.

While you're doing this, don't forget to identify positive feelings too. For example, if you go for a walk when it is snowing and let the flakes fall on your face, how does that make you feel? Say to yourself, "I feel _____ when snowflakes fall on my face." Get in touch with your feelings. Tell yourself that it is okay to feel.

Once you have learned to embrace your feelings, the next step is to learn to trust yourself. You might want to start by acting upon a feeling that you have. For example, if you've had a long, hard day at your work, but you can't go home for another hour, you may have the urge to step away from everything for a few minutes, maybe even step outside for a moment. Somehow, you feel it is extremely important to step away from your desk, just for five minutes. Trust that urge. Trust yourself to know what you need most at this moment. Get up from your desk and walk outside. Walk around the building, or stand at the door, allowing yourself to enjoy these precious minutes replenishing yourself.

After you start trusting yourself, you're ready to start building relationships of trust with others. Avoid building relationships with people who have the pieces you feel are lacking in yourself, and then working to control the other person. Build a relationship that allows the other person to be himself or herself.

Pick out someone you think you can trust, and then put yourself in a position of having to trust them. It may be something as simple as asking a person to pick up a sandwich for you. Start small in building trusting relationships. Take baby steps and learn from the falls along the way. For example, if your friend forgets to bring back the sandwich, resist the urge to say to yourself, "I knew it. Nobody can ever be trusted." Replace that negative talk with something like, "I understand now that she cannot be trusted to remember to bring me a sandwich, but that doesn't mean that I can't trust her in other ways."

Be careful, however, that you don't create tests for people to pass or fail. Give your trust freely in relationships. If someone lets you down, force yourself to remember that this doesn't mean that she is not worthy of your trust.

It might be helpful to observe how others trust people. You might even want to pick out a person you admire and use her as a role model. Watch how she interacts with others. How does she express her trust in others? How does she react when she is disappointed by others? How does she encourage others to be trustworthy and to trust her?

When you use a role model, you may find yourself wanting to behave in new ways. Don't fight this urge. Trust yourself! Change your behavior. Do things you have never done before. If, for example, you always keep your distance from others and never touch them, reach out (if it is appropriate) and lightly touch another person on the arm. It may seem uncomfortable at first. Identify that feeling. Validate it and embrace it. Trust it.

If you make a conscious effort to trust others, it won't be long before you feel something emerging within you. You'll feel a new sense of power, a new sense of who you are, a new sense of your personal identity. By following these steps, you'll re-create your personal boundaries. You will work through your feelings to build true limits for your personal space.

You'll grow beyond the emotional pain that controls your thinking. You'll grow beyond the need to use reprimands, put-downs and assassinations of character to control others. You'll no longer need to use shame and its companion — guilt — to get what you need in your relationships.

Manipulation Through Guilt

Guilt is often used in the workplace to manipulate others. It is a powerful and all too effective tool to control others.

While shame is a sense of being someone less than you should be, guilt is a sense that you have done something wrong. Guilt comes from the fear of failure. When you are afraid you might fail, you say things like "I can't," or "I wouldn't be good at that." Guilt manifests itself when you feel responsible for failures and shortcomings and are seduced by anyone's assertion that a "mistake" is your fault. You accept the guilty charge without reservation.

Guilt also relies on your sense of responsibility for others' emotions. If you feel powerless to fight back and suppress your own feelings, guilt grows.

When you are victimizing yourself, using statements like, "I couldn't help it," or "Why does this always happen to me?" you allow guilt to dominate your thinking and destroy your sense of self-worth.

When you say to others in a condescending tone, "How could you have let this happen?" you are provoking guilt. Because you have determined that your self-worth has been attacked, you are prepared to undermine others' self-worth. *Perpetual exposure to guilt destroys your sense of self-worth.*

Creating Self-Worth in Yourself and Others

We've seen how important it is that you send yourself messages that build your sense of self-worth, either through affirming messages or actions. The people you work with need these messages too. As a person who is working to reduce fear and anger, it is up to you to provide messages that increase the self-worth of those you work with. The people you work with need to hear that you hold them in high regard. They need to see by your actions that you trust and respect them. If this is uncomfortable for you, try using some of the following sample messages adapted by Jean Illsley from Clarke and Connie Dawson's book, *Growing Up Again, Parenting Ourselves, Parenting Our Children,* Harper/Hazelden © 1989.

"I'm glad you're in charge of that project."

"I know you will ask for help if it is needed."

"Your experience is valuable."

"I look forward to working with you."

"You can be responsible for your contributions to each of your commitments."

"Trust your intuition to help in making your decisions."

"It has been enjoyable to watch you initiate projects and grow."

"You can think before you say yes or no. It's okay to learn from your mistakes."

"It's all right to disagree."

"If you want to talk, I'm willing to listen."

"You're really a special person."

"I like working with you because you're so creative, competent, productive and joyful."

To create a strong, healthy sense of self-worth in yourself, use positive, affirming statements like these in your self-talk. Every morning, look at yourself in the mirror and say something nice to yourself. Tell yourself over and over that you are worthy and capable and a person you think is pretty nice to know.

Then share the message by building the self-worth of the people you work with. Liberally use affirming messages in your conversations with them. By helping others feel better about themselves, you will create a work environment where people feel valued and safe, a work environment where people can focus on their strengths instead of worrying about their fears.

By doing this, you will quickly learn that, indeed, "no man (or woman) is an island." You can never truly tame the dragons of fear and anger until you help others tame their dragons too.

The Myth of Independence

There is a myth in the workplace that in order to succeed you are supposed to be independent. You must *stand on your own* and *take care of your own problems.* You are told that it is unacceptable to allow personal problems to affect your job. Yet, everything you do is based on your personal perspective. If you feel fear, it will be reflected in the way you do your job and relate to others. If you feel that you have self-worth, that too will be reflected in the way you perform and relate to the people around you.

These people also feel fear and shame. They want recognition and security, too. And, like you, they always act out of a need for interdependence.

People often react to events in the workplace out of their fear-based needs. They become jealous over the advancement of others, sabotage individual or departmental plans or refuse to offer information.

There's a reason for all of this negative behavior. When you seek love and are turned away, or give love unquestioningly and are abused, you begin to question your trust in yourself and others. It hurts to participate and not be acknowledged for your ideas. It hurts to want recognition and receive only silence.

The Significance of Emotion

As a manager, you can help others come to terms with their emotions of fear and anger by recognizing their feelings. You can work with them to identify what they need from their jobs and from the people in the workplace. You can help them recognize the emotions and operational needs of others.

It is especially important to recognize feelings when there are conflicts because conflict is nothing more or less than a mix of emotion and information.

In normal conversations with others, you get things done by communicating what you need to other people. You pass along the information, and it is received with a minimum of emotion.

If you or the other person have strong emotions about the situation, however, the information being sent or received is filtered by emotion. Because emotion is filtering the flow of information, communication suffers. It becomes contaminated with information that may not be directly related to the issue. Indeed, this impaired communication makes it difficult for either of you to clearly identify the issues. If you were to build a formula for conflict, it would look like this:

Emotion   +   Disagreeing Information   =   Conflict

When conflict occurs, you have a different way of seeing things than your co-workers do. You attach different meanings to information. Your emotions blind you to the situation at hand, and make it hard to resolve the conflict. Or it may be resolved superficially, which only causes the emotions to intensify. To resolve a conflict, you must recognize and confront the emotional message coloring the information that is being exchanged.

Reaching Your Objectives

The goal of any conflict is to achieve a specific objective that is important to the people involved. Each person who is involved in the conflict feels that her objective is the best. They feel this way because of what they've learned from their experiences. And, as we have seen, the way they think about their experiences is colored by their emotions. The formula for reaching the objective might look like this:

Emotion   +   Thought   +   Experience   =   Objective

These are the essential elements that create your objectives. If you believe, based on the messages you assign to a particular experience, that you are "not capable," "you are not safe to feel," "you cannot learn new skills" or "you deserve what you get," then you get that same experience over and over. If your objective is to change your outcomes, you need to change your beliefs. By changing your beliefs, you will change your emotions and your thoughts. When you change your emotions and thoughts, you change your experience. It's not easy to do this, but if you truly want to increase your feelings of self-worth and stop repeating the same negative experiences again and again, work through these steps:

- Recognize and acknowledge positive emotions — what you want to feel. For example, acknowledge someone's trust as a positive, not a trap.

- Open your thinking so that other perspectives are possible. Take the time to understand where the other is coming from.

- Visualize the experience that creates opportunities for you. For example, visualize yourself working with more confidence and then *see* your boss giving you recognition for doing a good job.

- Allow a process to occur, rather than expect an event.

Exercise your skills in definition, clarity and balance by naming the emotions that you want connected with an experience. This act alone can alter your belief system.

For example, in your relationships, do you tend to give yourself internal statements such as these:

> *"I won't tell him this because he won't understand."*

> *"I'll just not tell the whole truth about this so there won't be an argument."*

> *"She's not capable of understanding this."*

These examples are colored by the belief that you cannot trust the other person with the truth. When you base your interaction with a person on this belief, you probably feel guarded. You feel that you have to be careful about what you say and how you say it. You don't trust the other person to take responsibility for her emotions about the information you give.

The fact is that you may be creating conflicts by withholding information and your true feelings. By taking responsibility for the other person's emotions, instead of simply speaking your own truth and letting an honest exchange occur, you may be setting the stage for conflict.

If you are not dealing honestly with another person — for their protection or your own — risk trusting them instead. Trust that you and the other person have the resources to work through any conflict.

Action Guidelines

1. Recognize your co-workers' need for appreciation, influence and justice.

2. Create an environment that feels safe for others and you.

3. Operate from honesty about your emotions.

4. Clarify to yourself your motivation for your words or actions. Deliver your words in a way that affirms others as well as yourself.

5. Silence is powerful. It can disarm others, destroy them or support them. Be careful how you apply it.

6. Remember important events that happen to your co-workers.

7. Provide a place for people to go to be by themselves.

8. Come to terms with your own emotions of fear and anger.

9. Monitor your intonation, eye movement and body language to be consistent with what you are saying.

10. Acknowledge interdependence in the workplace.

11. Alter your belief systems to be more positive.

3 WHAT YOUR DRAGON FEEDS ON

So the citizen held tight to the leash and gave it a tug. And then the dragon did the most incredible thing. It yawned! "I'm impressed," it said, looking at her with one yellow eye. "But if you don't mind, I think I'll have a bite to eat before we do battle." And the dragon reached behind itself and what it pulled out caused the citizen to begin trembling anew. There, in a pile, waiting to feed the dragon were the most horrible things. There was humiliation pie and ambiguous cake. A cauldron of anger bubbled on the back burner, while a bowl of mixed messages had been set out to rise. And serving it up was the most awful sight of all — a large, ragtag creature named Organizational Style.

Fear in the Workplace

Your job is your security. Your paycheck ensures your quality of life. Your job provides a major portion of your identity. It's what people often use to define who they are. Many times, your job provides a great deal of your social interaction. You make friends and enemies in your job. Your job gives a sense of purpose to your life.

All too often, though, you are acutely aware of the fragile thread that binds you to your job. You can lose your job through a whim of fate or an innocent misjudgment. Your company can fall on hard times and you may be on the list of those who must be "let go." You may fall on the wrong side of a political battle among the company ranks and suddenly find that your job is in jeopardy.

Or you may work for a person who believes that fear is a valuable tool in managing people, someone who thinks that instilling fear in people is the way to get them to work harder and longer. Managers who rely on fear to get work done generally invoke a great deal of anger in those who report to them. You can tell if this is your supervisor's management style — or worse, if this is your style of managing others — if any of the following patterns are present:

1. Ambiguity

2. Ineffective personnel systems

3. Unhealthy organizational style

Ambiguity

Ambiguity means never really knowing where you stand. People typically are ambiguous when they aren't sure about what they are doing and are afraid they will be "found out." Because they are unsure of the correctness of their decisions, they leave their actions and words open to others' interpretation. They protect themselves by never committing to a course of action or by changing their minds, depending upon who they talked with last.

When a manager is ambiguous, employees become insecure, fearful and angry. They are confused about what their priorities should be. Do you exhibit ambiguous behavior or experience it from others? Ask yourself if you exhibit these behaviors:

Do I exclude others from problem-solving or decision-making?

Do I avoid informing others of the decision-making process to be used?

Do I keep secrets or communicate indirectly?

Do I ask for feedback or suggestions and then not respond to them?

Do I give mixed or inconsistent messages — what applies to others doesn't apply to me, or vice versa?

Do I appear to be uncaring or indifferent?

Do I appear to be untrustworthy?

If these behaviors are part of your repertoire, then your fears are being fed. Also, it is possible that you are reacting to the ambiguous behavior of others. For example, the following edited letter was written by an employee to a manager. The behavior of the manager angered the employee. The letter illustrates the effect of ambiguous behavior from management to an employee.

Dear Manager,

At the last planning meeting for the upcoming project, I posed a legitimate question regarding how persons would be picked to facilitate meetings. I was told by you that you would answer my question after the meeting. You did not. Instead, nearly a month later, you called me asking if I might meet with you regarding my behavior, which you found unacceptable. Uncomfortable with walking into something as vague as what you were describing, I asked if you were taking me off the project.

You called back this morning and told me that was the case. I asked if this was negotiable, and you could not give me a straight answer; instead you asked me if I'd had difficulty in groups before. I am bringing this to your attention to register my deep disappointment in the tactics used.

Let me tell you what disturbs me about this the most. I was under the impression that you actually believed what you were talking about — developing partnerships in which the goal is a common good. That, above all, is what floors me about this!

I am attempting to be forthright, without blame, but what is a business doing talking about building workable relationships among people when it denies one of its employees those very opportunities? You have hurt me without having the decency to talk to me before making this decision. The innuendoes that you expressed on the phone this morning suggest that I am in the wrong.

If there is room for negotiation, I would be willing to partici-pate in your discussion. I do not consider my decision to be a lack of cooperation on my part, but I feel like I'm being victim-ized!

It is my deepest hope that this rift will work toward being something positive for both of us. I hope that you would be open to more than what you have presented about this situa-tion.

Sincerely,

The Employee

If you work for someone who exhibits ambiguous behavior, you might write your own letter and then use it for one of the following purposes:

- Do not send your letter. Use it solely for venting your anger.

- Now that you have defined your feelings in the letter, contact your manager and ask to meet and discuss your concerns.

- When you meet with your manager, resolve to listen as well as to talk. Try to clear your mind of preconceived messages based on your emotions about the situation. Express your willingness to understand the manager's viewpoint and your desire to work together. Ask your manager if he is interested in feedback on how you interpreted the process. If he says "yes," tell him tactfully and firmly what your feelings are.

By following this course of action, you can assist your manager in understanding the effect of his ambiguous behavior. In this way, you can assist in changing other people's behavior by first changing yours.

Ineffective Personnel Policies

Personnel policies generate fear and anger in the workplace when there are perceived inequities or unfairness in the treatment of employees. Those inequities may affect you directly or indirectly. When you see things happening to your co-workers that you think are unfair, you wonder if the same will happen to you. For example, if your manager talks to you about other employees when they are not present, you may wonder if he talks about you in the same way. If you are a manager and you talk about another employee without that employee being present, then the employee you're talking to probably wonders if you are talking about him when he is not present.

Fear is heightened in the workplace if personnel policies have only short-term benefits, or if follow-up that's promised never occurs. Some companies seem to change their policies as often as the weather. When you feel like you have to check the date on your latest memo to be sure you have the right information, you're always afraid that you will do something wrong.

Another example of ineffective personnel policies is a lack of interest on the part of management during employee tragedies, transitions or lay-offs. Some companies have an unwritten rule that it is inappropriate to talk about such personal things. Do they think no one notices what is happening around them?

It is also devastating when people receive mixed messages from the company. A good example of this is employee handbooks which say the company wants to promote from within its ranks, but available jobs are never posted for employees to see. To be effective, personnel policies must take into account the persons they are affecting.

Unhealthy Organizational Style

Every organization has its own style — its own unspoken, unwritten guidelines for proper behavior. Some organizations are very formal and hierarchical, requiring a certain code of dress and method of doing business within the business. Other organizations are more informal, with less rigid rules. Some organizations stress conformity while others stress creativity.

Whatever the "rules of conduct" are for your organization, they can either instill confidence in the people you work with or they can contribute to their fears. These traditions of proper conduct always come directly from top management. If top management encourages open communication and team effort, this will filter down to the lowest rung on the personnel ladder. On the other hand, if management perceives employees as enemies who must be controlled and manipulated, that is also how the employees will perceive management. In these instances, management usually becomes the enemy, and employees do everything they can to sabotage them — either through overt acts of destruction or through more indirect means of slacking off and doing only what has to be done to get by.

How we work together sets the tone for whether the organizational style will be healthy or unhealthy. What do you project? A healthy tone that encourages sharing information, finding strength in differences, speaking positively of others and willingness to work together? When you set the tone for positive qualities such as these, you are setting the stage for less fear and anger in the workplace. People begin to feel their needs are being addressed, and as a consequence, they renew their commitment to their work and their relationships.

Defining the Core Values of Your Organization

Defining the core values of an organization is imperative in these times of change. The future of organizations relies on developing core values that promote positive assumptions, relationships, structures and roles. If your organization is not willing to review what it really cares about, it may lock itself into perpetual patterns of fear. These unhealthy patterns are akin to the ones described earlier in the Circle of Shame that occurs within an individual. Like one individual caught in this cycle, the organization relies on negative assumptions and behavioral patterns that destroy trust.

Discover the core values that are needed in your workplace by asking the people you work with these questions:

> *"What are the characteristics of a good team, an effective partnership or a positive working relationship?"*

> *"What are the qualities that are important in a positive relationship?"*

> *"What needs to happen here at work to create positive working relationships?"*

These basic questions will help you gather information for defining the core values of your organization and identifying how the organization can be structured to meet the needs of the employees. A healthy and productive work environment results when inner needs are met. Conversely, *if inner needs are not satisfied, organizational restructuring or increased communication will not feel like enough.*

Shift Assumptions to the Positive

When you are defining the core values of your company, work to be sure they are positive, nurturing and productive values that build respect among all people. When you feel frustrated with an employee, you probably ask yourself, *"Why do I have to deal with this employee? He never gives me a straight answer, just excuses. He doesn't understand the concept of team. He doesn't care about this job or the people he works with. I can't trust him to do his job. He is not responsible."*

If you feel this way about an employee and you lack the value of respect, your conversations with him will be colored by your belief that this person is unreliable and uncaring. Your dialogue may become condescending. Your anger will show in your words and action. You may even stop responding to him because you have already determined that he is untrustworthy.

If this occurs, it is important to ask yourself, "How does this person perceive me as his manager?" What are the real issues in your relationship with this person? Is one real issue the negative belief you have that you cannot trust this person?

Based on what you've seen and experienced, you may feel you know what is motivating him: *"He only wants to make my life miserable."* That is your perception of reality. To act in a way that is contrary to this belief means you have to change. Change means taking risks, and nothing is more risky than changing interpersonal relationships.

In order to grow beyond your negative belief, however, you have to identify and clarify your assumptions. Ask yourself if your assumptions come from limited, self-defeating thoughts. If they do, try to shift your thinking to encompass positive, productive thoughts.

An amazing thing happens when you operate from a core belief in positive assumptions about people. Quite often, people change. If you believe someone is trustworthy, he becomes more trustworthy. If you believe he is out to make your life miserable, you can be assured that he will do so.

The bottom line is that people all want the same thing. You want to feel connected to others, and so do the people who work with and for you. You want to take pride in the company you work for and feel that you are a part of a good organization. So do the people around you. You want to feel that others care about your feelings. So do the people you work with.

A Positive Assumption About Anger in the Workplace

If you look honestly within yourself and at the people you work with, you'll see that anger is all around you. It's there when people work through their disagreements and fears. It's there when management sends mixed messages. It's there when people try to control others.

Acknowledge your feelings of anger by truly seeing other people's struggles. And remember that people get angry with people and situations they care about. If it wasn't important to them or interfering with their goals, people would become irritated, but not angered.

If people are angry in your workplace, they are sending a message — and that message is a cry for recognition and respect.

Action Guidelines

1. Make a commitment to create a safe and effective environment.

2. Clarify your perceptions of your own behavior.

3. Model the behavior you want to happen in the workplace.

4. Change your assumptions. Ask questions about fear.

5. Ask for feedback, and ask if others want feedback.

6. Monitor your personal changes.

7. Encourage others to make decisions. Demonstrate shared power.

8. Focus on the present and the future.

9. Facilitate dialogue and encourage involvement in problem-solving.

10. Invite ideas and activities from outside resources.

4 TAKING A STAND WITH THE DRAGON

And then Revelation came to the citizen. It drew her aside and whispered in her ear. "I come to tell you a secret," it said in a gentle voice. "I need all the help I can get," the citizen conceded. "Are you afraid of the dragon?" Revelation asked. "I may be powerless, but I'm not stupid," the citizen retorted. "Of course I'm afraid of the dragon." Revelation looked at her for a long time ... so long that the citizen became uneasy. Meanwhile, the dragon, bored by all the goings-on, decided to take a little nap and started snoring. "You said you are powerless," Revelation said. "Do you believe that is true?" The citizen nodded. "There is the secret you need to know," Revelation said. "The dragon has put a spell on you to blind you to what you are. Don't you see? The power is within you. The power IS you."

How to Recognize Your Power

When you hear the word *power*, what do you think? Many times, power is viewed as something bad: *"Power means control, someone telling me what to do."* Like anger, it is often misunderstood and misused. If you don't consider it bad, then you may think it is something *so* good that you become enamored with it or self-absorbed with the influence *you* have and the changes *you* create. When this occurs, you pridefully say, *"Look what I can do."* Most of us have experienced the abuse of power. You may have had it modeled for you throughout your life. You, in turn, then misuse your power because you think that's its purpose.

What does it really mean to be powerful? Remember the commercial, *"When E. F. Hutton talks, people listen"*? That's an example of power— valuable information about making money in exchange for money. TV programs like *Dallas* and *Dynasty* were blunt examples of the misuse of power. People used their knowledge of others to get what they wanted. Millions of viewers enjoy watching other people succeed or be destroyed. They think they are vicariously feeling what power is when, in reality, they are watching the misuse of power.

True power is not what you have. Power is your ability to influence, your ability to choose consciously, your ability to be responsible.

The power that is within you is infinite. There is an endless supply. When you deny your power, you cut it off and become exhausted, lose hope and reinforce your negative beliefs about yourself and others. To feel powerless is to feel discounted, dismissed, used, taken advantage of, minimized, devalued and invalid. You think no one cares about you, your thoughts or your feelings and that others count more than you. Powerlessness requires a victim.

The Tools of Power

We all have a lot of power tools, and like with any tool, you can either use them or abuse them. Your personal arsenal of power includes such things as:

- *Knowledge* — you know something (and someone else doesn't)

- *Information* — you will give it (but only if you benefit)

- *Guilt* — you know a co-worker responds to guilt (so you use it)

- *Hierarchy* — you are management (and only you make the rules and the decisions)

- *Personality* — your presence makes someone uncomfortable (and you take advantage)

- *Age* — you're more experienced (and that makes you better)

- *Financial* — you make more money (and that means you're more important)

- *Group identity* — your gender makes up the majority of the employees (and what the group determines is right)

- *Reward or punishment* — you are able to reward or not (and get what you want)

By recognizing your behavior patterns, you can learn to use your power in ways that are effective and help those around you grow. To discover how you use your power, listen to yourself speak. Observe others and listen to what they say. You will see how ineffective, unclear communication can lead you into a drama where events take on an importance that is out of proportion. Within this drama you may fear loss of control. If the need for control becomes heightened, you may even live for the exciting energy that is produced.

If you are in this kind of situation, you may have developed a habit of gaining power through indirect communication. Rather than confront the person with whom you have concerns, you tell someone else who gives you sympathy. You feel more powerful for the moment, but you haven't done anything to remedy your problems.

Drama Triangle Effect

A tool that can help you see the *what, how and why* of what you say is the *Drama Triangle* invented by Stephen Karpman. The following information on the Drama Triangle is adapted from *Cathexis Reader: Transactional Analysis Treatment of Psychosis* by J. I. Schih, N.Y. Harper & Row Publishers, Inc. 1975. The Drama Triangle was created to help identify unproductive psychological games and better understand personal power. It also demonstrates how the need for control is created. On the three corners of the triangle are the roles of *Persecutor, Rescuer and Victim*. The Victim is the key to the interchange among the three players. As long as someone is willing to be a Victim the drama continues. If you participate in the drama as Persecutor or Rescuer, eventually you become the Victim. In actuality, all players in this drama feel like Victims. Persecutors and Rescuers think their roles give them power, because the energy that is created is stimulating, but unproductive. The ups and downs of the drama are emotionally charged and addictive.

There are exceptions to the Drama Triangle. Real victims, real rescuers and real persecutors exist. You can be a victim without playing the drama, and you are not necessarily part of the triangle every time you rescue someone. However, whenever you persecute, you may promote this unproductive psychological game.

A Drama Triangle

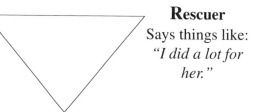

Persecutor
Says things like:
*"She's going to
pay for this!"*

Rescuer
Says things like:
*"I did a lot for
her."*

Victim
Says things like:
*"She did this to me, and now
there's nothing I can do."*

In order for you to shift from this structure to one of problem-solving, you need to check out your feelings. You need to ask yourself the following questions (adapted from information by Jean Illsley Clarke in *Who, Me Lead A Group?* published by Harper Collins © 1984):

What am I feeling?

How can I use these feelings to understand my behavior?

What do I really want?

How can I best get there and benefit everyone concerned in this?

Is there anyone who can help me understand, or solve this?

17

These questions help you shift from feeling powerless to feeling empowered, from being a Victim to becoming a Problem-Solver. They help you break the addictive energy that keeps you in the drama and shift from Persecutor to Structurer, from Rescuer to Nurturer. Your new monologue could follow this model:

The Winning Option

**From Victim to
Problem-Solver**

Says things like:
*"What options are available
to solve this? This looks
crippling, but I can work
this through if I slow down."*

**From Rescuer
to Nurturer**

Says things like:
*"It seems like I want ... If I
look at these options, I could
consider this or that. I could
run these ideas past my
trusted friend, Judy."*

**From Persecutor
to Structurer**

Says things like:
*"This is what I can now
expect. This is what it will
mean to me. I need to
understand this situation,
and I will need to speak with
Gloria when I am clear
about my anger."*

Shifting to Positive Power

You stop the drama when you become conscious of how your fear and anger control you. When you are angry, you are armed for the attack. When you are afraid, you easily misuse your power. Stop the drama by thinking what you would automatically say. *Then responsibly say* what would be empowering for yourself and others. With practice, you will stop thinking in fear-based responses. Your empowering statements will become automatic. To see how this works, let's look at how Julie handles a difficult situation. She is facilitating a meeting and Joan keeps interrupting her.

> ***Julie the Victim thinks:*** *"How did I get stuck in this facilitator's role? This is too hard. I can't stop this."*

> ***Julie the Problem-Solver says:*** *"Will you give me your attention, please? We only have a half hour remaining, and we have several agenda items left for discussion. What items require decisions or discussion at this time? With that clarified, I encourage your suggestions and action on ...."*

Julie has taken action to control the meeting in a manner that will be beneficial to all. However, Joan is persistent and she interrupts again.

> ***Julie the Persecutor thinks:*** *"Give me a break, Joan. You know better than this. Why don't you just back off, and let other people speak for a change?"*

> ***Julie the Structurer says:*** *"Joan, several people have not been able to contribute to the discussion because of these interruptions. Please, state your concerns and then let's hear what concerns others have regarding this issue. Each of you will be asked if you want to contribute. Thank you."*

Julie continues the meeting. By now, Joan has taken the hint and is allowing others to speak. However, Julie, afraid that Joan is being silent because she is angry, now takes on a new role in the drama.

Julie the Rescuer thinks: *"Poor Joan, I can see that it is really hard for her to wait to talk. Maybe I was too rough on her."*

Julie the Nurturer says: *"Joan, if there is something that you need from us, we will listen as soon as Alice finishes expressing her concerns."*

Using Your Personal Power to Move from Victim to Problem-Solver

By consciously acting as a Problem-Solver, Structurer and Nurturer, you give others the opportunity to act in responsible ways. Each of these roles has its own characteristics, language and benefits.

The Victim feels helpless, discounted and powerless. If you are operating as a Victim, you blame others and indulge in self-pity. You deny your feelings and hold others responsible for your happiness or unhappiness. If you change your role from Victim to Problem-Solver, you immediately begin to use your power. The Problem-Solver is able to work through the problem and be creative. As a Problem-Solver, you take responsibility for your actions and their outcome. You acknowledge your feelings and integrate them into your actions.

The Victim says: *"I couldn't help it. It will never change."* The Problem-Solver says: *"What are my options? Can my feelings give me clues?"* The Victim feels powerful when manipulating others to take care of her. The Problem-Solver feels powerful when taking personal responsibility.

Using Your Power to Move from Persecutor to Structurer

Dramatic differences can also be seen between the Persecutor and the Structurer. When you are in the Persecutor role, you believe that others must do what you want them to do. You blame others for the anger and stress that you feel. You ignore the needs of others because you believe that no one else cares about the problem as much as you do.

When you release yourself from the Persecutor role and become a Structurer, you use your personal power to resolve the problem. You set and meet expectations. You show concern for your own safety and that of others. You work to create an environment where everyone can be effective.

A typical Persecutor statement goes like this: *"I am right and you're wrong. You will pay for this. You don't have what it takes. Give me that and I will do it!"*

A Structurer would say: *"What agreements do we need so we can work together? I understood that we agreed to handle it this way, but you appear to have a different perspective. If you tell me what you are thinking, we can build a stronger relationship. We all have valuable perspectives."*

A Persecutor feels powerful when blame is focused on others. A Structurer feels powerful when everyone knows what is expected and is responsible for their actions.

To move from Persecutor to Structurer, ask yourself what it would feel like to share your power. What would happen? How would you behave and encourage others to take more power?

Second, ask yourself what you're going to do if you're not right. Will you get defensive? Will you be able to say, "You know, I think I might be wrong"? What is the worst that could happen if you should be wrong? Would you be fired? Would people laugh at you? How would you handle being wrong with dignity and power?

Third, imagine what it would feel like to have commitment and cooperation from others. Would it be comfortable for you? Would you be able to release enough control to allow others to come forth? How could you gain cooperation and commitment from others? And fourth, ask yourself what you can learn from others about yourself.

After you have examined your feelings, ask others what agreements they need to work more effectively. What do they need from you? What do they need from other people in the group? How do they want to structure your work relationship?

Ask them if anyone has any special agendas that need to be addressed. What are going to be the rules of conduct in the group? Would they like to have a highly structured group or a more informal one? Establish the parameters for working together.

Then ask everyone in the group to share their expectations of the other people in the group and the roles they think will be needed. Ask them what the consequences should be if agreements are broken.

Using Your Power to Move from Rescuer to Nurturer

Moving out of the Rescuer mode and into that of the Nurturer can be the most difficult of all. Rescuing others is a subtle form of power and can be highly addictive. If you are in the Rescuer mode, you feel you must take care of others. You believe that others cannot solve their own problems, and you hide your own feelings, thinking you are doing the "noble" thing. If someone asks if you need help, you'll likely say "no," even though you may need it. Often, if you are being a Rescuer, you feel superior.

If you move into the Nurturer mode, however, you support others, but you don't feel responsible for their feelings and actions. You believe others can solve their own problems. You spend more time listening to people than trying to fix their problems for them. You acknowledge people for themselves.

A Rescuer says things like: *"Oh, you didn't know any better. I'll take care of everything."*

A Nurturer says: *"I care for you. You are able to handle this. What kind of help do you need from me so you can resolve this?"*

Rescuers feel powerful because they are needed and in control. Nurturers feel powerful because their support assists others in solving their problems.

To move from Rescuer to Nurturer, ask yourself:

1. What feelings am I denying or trying to avoid? How can I address these feelings?

2. If I stopped trying to fix the situation, what would happen? What does that mean to me?

3. What are my expectations for myself?

4. What do I want from the person whom I am trying to rescue?

And then, ask others:

1. What are you willing to do about this situation?

2. What has been your involvement in resolving this situation?

3. How can I assist you in resolving your dilemma?

4. What are you expecting from me?

The Winning Option

By choosing to be responsible in your interpersonal relationships, you are moving out of the Drama Triangle and into the Winning Option. You are being responsible for how you use your power, and your ability to influence, not to control. To move into the Winning Option is to open the door to growth for yourself and others.

Your power is revealed in your behavior, your words and your intentions. You know your power by acknowledging your feelings and learning from them. Embrace your power. When people can see the power in you, you encourage the power in them. Through the conscious choice of empowering others, you become empowered yourself.

Action Guidelines

1. Determine how you use your power.

2. Recognize how your fear and anger are controlling you.

3. Listen to others and yourself. What is your language telling you? Are you willing to be a Problem-Solver?

4. Use your power to empower others.

5. Be responsible with your power by helping others make their own decisions and choices.

5 DRAWING OUT THE DRAGON

And so the citizen turned back to the dragon, armed with a new sense of her own power. "I know that you're big and strong," she said. "I know that you have many weapons. But since we both live here, we need to communicate with each other." The dragon snorted and looked at her with contempt. "Why should I do anything a weak creature like you wants me to do?" it asked. "Because," she said, "you live in my heart and my heart is changing. Don't you feel the walls of your dark cave getting smaller as my heart grows stronger?" And the dragon looked around and saw that what she said was true. "Come with me," she said gently. "Let us find a new place where we can work out our differences."

Fear and Anger in Relationships

Good working relationships require the fostering of mutual growth. You want relationships that build your sense of self-worth. However, you may unconsciously slip into dramas of fear and anger that break down relationships and cause you great pain. You may get trapped in negative scenarios because on some level, there is a pay-off for you. You feel an emotional gain.

Deep down, things are not working for you. Even when you win, you feel dissatisfied. You feel fearful and angry. You are creating poor relationships at your own expense.

Whether you know it or not, you are experiencing a crisis. Your challenge is to recognize that crisis. When you say to yourself, *"I am no longer willing to be unworthy,"* your crisis becomes a birth. You discover a new perspective. You see how unproductive the old ways of relating are. You begin to design new structures for your relationships as the old ones disintegrate. It is at this moment that you become open to possibilities. You learn to operate from the premise that everyone has something to contribute. There are no enemies. You understand that you must rely on yourself and your co-workers, and that it is important that everyone feels emotionally safe and secure. You take responsibility for your part in making sure that happens for everyone. You encourage your co-workers to contribute to the process.

The Structure You Need in Relationships

For relationships to develop, they need communication and structure. Communication provides an opportunity to hear, understand and feel differences and commonalities, while the way you share interpretations, assumptions and perceptions provides the structure. When structured communications are used skillfully, fear and anger are lessened.

Structure is especially important in determining the type of relationships you have. Even if you feel there is too much structure at your workplace, for instance, that structure gives you a sense of security. Because you have structure, you know what to expect.

Building on what others expect, on their structure, is thus an effective way to present new ideas. For example, let's say your company has a particular form for ordering supplies, but the accounting department has decided that the form needs to be changed to better meet their requirements. One way of presenting the changes might be to incorporate new lines on the old forms, rather than creating a totally new form.

Identifying the Structure in Your Workplace

Structure is the accepted process that you and your co-workers use to solve problems. Ask yourself these questions to help see the structure you use:

How do interchanges occur within my workplace?

Do I have regular, routine meetings? Hallway encounters? Secret sessions?

Am I asked to discuss issues with my staff? Do I ask others to meet with us?

Do I schedule these meetings or are they spontaneous? What is my pattern?

Have I changed my way of doing things in the recent past? How did I change?

Do I find myself always using the same mechanism to explore people's ideas?

Whenever you want to change a structure, be sure to analyze what has been accepted as the "right" way to do things, and then make sure that everyone understands the reasons for the change. That's true for changes in the structure of relationships as well as within the workplace.

Your Options for Solving Problems

There are as many different ways to handle problems as there are people. To be sure that you are responding to problems instead of reacting to them, use the *ACE Analysis* to help you select your best option for problem-solving.

Your first option is to *Avoid* it. After analyzing the problem, you may decide that the benefits of solving it are not significant. Or the costs are too great, and the potential damage of exploring it is too much for you. The goals may not be well defined, and its importance to the relationship is not obvious. You need time, so you withdraw.

Another option is to *Confront* it. You confront it when the relationship really matters. Your goals include the maintenance of the relationship or the redefining of goals. You need to know what is going on, because this relationship affects your future.

A third option is to *Explore* it. When the relationship has potential, together you find out what has caused the uncomfortable interchange. You problem-solve with the other person and allow yourselves to discover new goals.

Types of Structure for Problem-Solving

If you choose to confront or explore, then you need to look at the different structures that can be implemented to draw upon the experiences and talents of your co-workers so they feel empowered to make their own decisions and to do their own problem-solving. Three types of structures to consider are Self-Help Decision-Making, Assisted Decision-Making and Third-Party Decision-Making.

Self-Help Decision-Making

This structure allows everyone to contribute to the problem-solving process. Everyone's idea has equal weight. Models for self-help decision-making include:

Information Meetings — informal meetings to exchange information.

Dialogues — informal sharing of inner thoughts and feelings that may or may not apply directly to decisions, but give greater understanding of the assumptions from which each person operates.

Conciliation — sharing information and resources so the participants settle through self-negotiation.

Collaborative Problem-Solving — learning the skills for decision-making and working together to apply a step-by-step process that the participants agree upon.

Negotiations — allows individuals to develop agreements between themselves.

Assisted Decision-Making

This structure is best used when there is a need to improve the skills of other people, when trying to resolve differences, or when providing information when you are not responsible for the final decision. Models for assisted decision-making include:

Counseling or therapy, team-building, informal social activities, partnering, coaching, training, facilitation, mediation, convenor, ombudsman, mini-trial, dispute panels, advisory mediation, fact finding or settlement conferences.

Third-Party Decision-Making

This structure is best used in situations calling for unbiased, impartial decisions to be made by an uninvolved third party. Models for third-party decision-making include:

Non-binding arbitration, summary jury trial, voting, binding arbitration, mediation then arbitration, binding disputes panels, private courts or litigation.

Of these three structures, the self-help approaches offer the greatest flexibility and effectiveness in the workplace. Two self-help decision-making models — the A.C.E.S. Problem-Solving Model, and the Four-Step Problem-Solving Model — are very simple to apply, but they approach problem-solving from very different perspectives.

A.C.E.S. Problem-Solving Model

The emphasis in this model is on getting in touch with the feelings behind the situation and encouraging dialogue through the following four actions:

Assessing needs by asking:

> What do I believe?
>
> What do I want?
>
> What do I love?
>
> What do I fear?

Controlling direction by:

> Identifying the fear and anger.
>
> Keeping your perspective.
>
> Using emotions in a positive way.
>
> Watching for patterns.

Engaging others by:

> Admitting to yourself and the other party the reality of the current situation.
>
> Identifying your self-centered choices.
>
> Deciding to put the needs of the other person ahead of yours.

Solving differences by:

> Avoiding arguing for your own individual judgment.
>
> Assuming that everyone can win.
>
> Staying true to your principles.
>
> Avoiding resolution techniques such as majority vote, averaging or splitting the difference.
>
> Using smaller groups to address problems.
>
> Expecting differences of opinion — they are only natural.

The Four-Step Problem-Solving Model

This model focuses on the problem more than the emotions behind the problem. It relies upon solving the problem by following these four steps:

>   *1. **Identify*** the problem by diffusing the emotions and clarifying the disagreement.
>
>   *2. **Focus*** on the problem by exploring mutual concerns, by determining shared needs and by thinking about the future.
>
>   *3. **Problem Solve*** creatively by discovering the things you and others care about, by utilizing brainstorming techniques working from an ideal situation.
>
>   *4. **Resolve*** the problem by determining the consequences of the options, evaluating the advantages and disadvantages of the options and developing agreements that are realistic in meeting everyone's needs.

However you choose to solve problems, the structure needs to be clarified and agreed upon prior to beginning the process. Once people know what to expect, they feel safe and are more willing to express themselves. However, if people don't agree with the structure, they may agree to work things through but not be satisfied with the results. A key to getting people to be satisfied and *buy-in* to the process is to ask for their input. People support what they help to create. Draw upon the resources around you. Ask questions and let people develop the structure that everyone can live with.

Three Styles for Handling Problems

Once you have agreed upon a process for solving problems, you then need to determine the style to implement it. Three distinctive styles are:

- *Directive* — This is a controlling style. Its message is "We know the process, tell us your thoughts." The person who directs is the most actively involved.

- *Therapeutic* — This is a sensitive style. Its message is, "How do you feel about that?" The style calls for responsiveness to individuals' feelings.

- *Humanistic* — This is an honoring style. Its message is, "What wisdom can each of us draw on?" This style empowers all involved parties.

As a manager, you can choose a style to present a particular process or adapt the styles to differing circumstances. You have choices, lots of them. All of these possible structures give you the means for sharing perceptions and interpretations within groups and lessening fear and anger in the workplace.

Action Guidelines

1. Strive to develop an atmosphere for mutual growth.

2. Put aside your own needs to share perceptions and assumptions.

3. Provide people with structure.

4. Implement models that create positive change.

5. Be sensitive to how you deliver structure.

6. Remember you always have choices in how to handle situations.

6 COMMUNICATING WITH THE DRAGON

The dragon followed the citizen out to the new place she had created for it, and then it drew back. "Why are you doing this?" it asked. "Is this some trick you've devised?" The citizen looked at the dragon and sighed. "Don't you see?" she said. "All I want to do is talk to you. I want to hear what you have to say." "Why?" asked the dragon warily. "How can I know your power if you don't tell me?" the citizen asked, an innocent look on her face. The dragon studied her, torn between its reservations and its conceit. As its conceit won out, the citizen struggled not to laugh. For you see, the citizen knew, deep in her heart, that communication was the key to controlling her dragon at last.

Patterns of Communication

The way you communicate plays a key role in your relationships. Your patterns of communication can either induce or reduce fear and anger in others.

When you communicate, you are both sending and receiving information. And the information you are sending goes far beyond the words you are speaking. Studies show that the majority of the information you communicate comes not from your words, but rather from your tone of voice and the body language you use when you are interacting with another person. You might say, for example, "Have a nice day" to someone. If you have a look of concern on your face and lean towards the person while you say these words, you are sending an entirely different message than if you say them while glaring at the person and moving away.

Conversely, the information you receive while communicating can have a significant impact on the communication. For example, if you are talking to someone who appears to be hanging on your words, you are more likely to feel confident enough to share with them. If you are talking to someone who appears to be disinterested, disdainful, or openly hostile toward you, you are likely to feel fear and anger. Your communication and willingness to share will dramatically change. The underlying motive behind your communication will be to leave this painful situation as soon as possible.

Communication is an important key in understanding the fear and anger that people feel. To communicate effectively with others, you need several skills. The key skill you need to develop, however, is the skill of listening.

Six Ways to Listen Effectively

Listening is more than sitting back and letting the other person speak while you decide what you are going to say next. You have to listen not only to what the speaker is saying, but also to the message behind the words.

There are six keys to listening more effectively: body language, reflective listening, paraphrasing, summarizing, openness and agreement statements.

Body Language

The first key to effective listening is to use your body to convey the message "I'm listening." You do this by giving your full attention to the speaker. Maintain eye contact, nodding your head at appropriate times and turning your body toward the person who is speaking, leaning slightly forward. Say things such as "I see," "OK," "uh huh," "really" or "oh." All of these are signals that you are interested in listening to the other person — that you are "there."

Reflective Listening

The second key to effective listening is reflective listening. When you are listening reflectively, you repeat a word or phrase spoken by the person who is speaking. Like a mirror, you reflect back to the speaker what she has said. By mirroring back part of what was spoken, you direct the conversation without interference by encouraging her to be more specific. You then gather the information you need to understand what the speaker is trying to say.

Example:

> Speaker: *"That Becky is a snake. She took credit for all the work that was done on the conversion project. In my presence, she told the consultant it was her idea and her development!"*

> Listener: *"She took all the credit?" "She told the consultant it was her idea?"*

Paraphrasing

Closely related to reflecting is the third listening skill — paraphrasing. Paraphrasing means restating what another person has said in your own words. This is one of the most powerful skills that you can use.

Example:

> Speaker: *"How am I supposed to get the report done, continue with the client survey, respond to the complaint calls on the fiasco from yesterday and revise the schedule for what will certainly be another mistake this next week? This kind of pressure is pushing me to the edge!"*

> Listener: *"You must be terrified about not being able to handle all the things you've been asked to do."*

> Speaker: *"Terrified. You can say that again. I just don't want to be in a situation like last year when I got really sick for two months. I am not good at juggling a variety of things. 'Keep it where I can handle it' is my motto."*

Listener: *"You sound like you would feel more sure of yourself if you were handling similar projects."*

Speaker: *"Wouldn't that be the day! I don't see that coming for a long time."*

Listener: *"You must feel concern over the workload assignments, the effort it takes to shift from one project to the next at a moment's notice and the effect that it's having on you physically. Is that what you're saying? In response to that, I'm willing to discuss the assignments that are given to people here. It may not mean less work, but, perhaps, there is a way to get things done that would help all of us feel more secure during these busy times. I will put the topic of discussing assignments on the agenda for our staffing next week. Do you think this will bring us closer to meeting your concern?"*

In paraphrasing, you can also respond with:

"I want to make sure I understand. You're upset about all the work ..."

If people feel differently, they will correct you. *"Not upset, just plain scared that I'm going to run myself down physically."*

"So the way you see it, the workload is burdening you ..."

People let you know if you are hearing what they are saying. *"Right, a burden."*

"You are very unhappy with handling calls from customers with complaints."

By picking out one piece of information, you are asking for clarification. The speaker responds, *"It's not the calls. It's the shifting gears from writing, to statistics, to complaints. I'm not good at changing so quickly."*

"You are angry about the amount of work ..."

Changing the focus a bit on the same general information, you again ask for clarification. The speaker responds, *"Yeah, I'm angry about having to do this. But really, I'm scared that I just can't perform to your standards."*

When you listen to people, you will hear their deepest fears and the reasons for their anger. Paraphrasing can bring this to the surface. It makes these emotions available to be understood. *In paraphrasing, you defuse the feelings by acknowledging the person and validating the emotions without judgment.* These could be feelings that people may have been denying for a lifetime. As you paraphrase, you help people define themselves. You help them understand their emotions and what their emotions are telling them. Also, you gain a greater understanding of what happened or is happening. You clarify and summarize that communication so both of you understand.

Five Keys in Paraphrasing

Skillful paraphrasing requires practice. When you emphasize the speaker's feelings and clarify the information he is giving you, you make an immediate connection with that person. The speaker feels heard and understood. You discover what she is really talking about, and you see more clearly the real motivations of your co-workers or employees.

To build your skill in paraphrasing, follow these steps:

1. Focus on the speaker's experience, not yours. Your experiences and feelings are not part of the equation for the moment. Strive to understand what is being said by the other person.

2. Restate what the other person says in your own words.

3. Acknowledge both the feelings and the facts. Sometimes people will never mention a feeling, but their body language and tone of voice will give you clues. Allow people to test their emotional reality by pulling out a feeling from what was said.

For example, you might say things like:

> *"You're angry that Jim is so insensitive to your requests."*

> *"You're annoyed that this happens."*

> *"Are you hurt by Judy's behavior?"*

Remember that some people may have difficulty with acknowledging the feeling you identify. If you sense this is the case, shift your focus from feelings to the information and use phrases such as:

> *"So you believe very strongly that ..."*

> *"The way you see it then ..."*

4. Be empathetic, not judgmental. Don't say: *"Well, if it were me, I'd ..."* *"How could you let them do that! Can't you stand up for yourself?"*

   Do say: *"I can understand why you're angry about the dismissal of your idea ..."*

5. Be brief. You only need to touch on a feeling that you believe is there along with some of the information. This alone is a signal that you are really interested, and it does not interrupt the other person's conversation.

Summarizing

The fourth step to effective listening is to restate the other person's key points. Identify the general ideas. *In effective summarizing, you control the issues and work toward problems that can be solved.* The emotions have been validated and moved out of the communication.

For example, you could say things like:

"To summarize the main points, I understand that ..."

"Let's see, so far we have discussed these particular areas of concern ... Is there any concern that was overlooked or needs to be clarified?"

The value of summarizing is that it not only communicates that you have been listening, but also provides a basis for moving forward and taking action.

Openness

To communicate that you are listening, you also can use openness in your conversation. Openness indicates to others that you are interested in hearing more about their perceptions and needs. You express openness by making statements such as:

"Say more about ..."

"Tell me what you have on your mind ..."

"Give me a specific example ..."

Openness is an especially effective listening skill to use when people are being critical or competitive. It signals your willingness to move beyond feelings and into problem-solving.

Agreement Statements

No matter how much you disagree with what someone is saying, you can always find something in the conversation that you can agree with. If you acknowledge where you agree with the other person, even while involved in a disagreement, you will diffuse much of the emotion that colors the conversation. It is hard to be angry with someone who agrees with you. It is easier to problem-solve when there is potential for agreement. Agreement statements begin like this:

"I agree with you that ..."

"I can see what you're saying about ..."

"I share your concerns about ..."

Powerful Speaking Methods

In communication, listening skills are valuable in providing an avenue to nurturing and problem-solving, while speaking skills assist in problem-solving. Effective speaking skills allow you to state what your intention is, what you need, how you feel and what an event means to you. Powerful speaking skills include speaking up, "I" messages, intention statements and preference statements.

Speaking Up

It is important for you to express your needs and concerns in the workplace. If you fear that you will say the wrong thing, begin with short sentences that express what happened. Stick to the facts first, then gradually introduce how you feel. Others will know what your ideas are only if you express them. When you talk about what is inside you, then people will know what matters to you and can act on your information.

"I" Messages

This is a speaking skill that allows you to share your feelings and concerns without blaming or criticizing others. "I" messages show that you are willing to take responsibility for your own emotions. In "I" messages, you speak for yourself, recognize emotion but not behavior and identify your own emotional needs.

"I" messages help you manage your feelings and information by expressing them in a nonjudgmental way. When a person does something that makes you feel a certain way — angry, frustrated, excited, joyful — you want to express yourself *so your feelings will be understood and so the other person can do something about what you are saying*. An "I" message is different than a "You" message. "You" messages put people on the defensive and make them feel you are attacking them. "You" messages sound like this:

>*"You know better than that."*

>*"You made me get a reprimand."*

>*"You're stupid and disgusting."*

On the other hand, "I" messages identify your emotions and limit arguments to the issues. Although the receivers may not welcome the "I" message, they are more likely not to view it as a personal attack.

To use an "I" message, identify (a) the action that bothered you, (b) the feeling it evoked in you and (c) the consequences that action produced for you.

The "I" message can be delivered in the order of A + B + C, with "A" being "What happened," "B" being "How I feel," and "C" being, "How it affects me."

Diagram of an "I" Message

A	B	C
What Happened	**How I Feel**	**How It Affects Me**
Describe the behavior and don't blame: *"When the report was not turned in on time ..."*	State your feelings about the possible consequences: *"I get upset ..."*	State the consequences: *"Because then I'm put in a difficult position with the committee."*

The "I" message confronts the other person by focusing on the impact of the situation on the speaker's emotions or performance.

Intention Statements

Intention statements are a third powerful speaking skill. These are statements that give others information about you — what is important to you, who you are, and if possible, how they can help you achieve your goal. Intention statements are useful because they minimize misunderstandings. An intention statement might sound like this:

> *"My intention in telling you this is that deadlines are crucial, and we need to talk about how deadlines can be met."*

> *"I'm trying to create a timetable for the submission of reports that everyone can meet."*

> *"I'm in the process of reviewing the reporting requirements, and I need your assistance."*

When you make an intention statement, be sure that your message is clear by using very specific, nonjudgmental language. The basis of all intention statements is your trust that others are willing to cooperate and work together in good faith. The power of the intention statement is its lack of manipulative ploys to coerce others to do what you want.

Preference Statements

Preference statements communicate your preferences or needs without stating them as demands or forcing others to guess what you want. These statements might sound like this:

> *"I would like to receive your individual suggestions, and then we'll see if we can generate a further list of creative options."*

> *"My preference is that our discussions remain confidential."*

> *"It would be helpful to me if you could let me know if you are having difficulty with the reports at least a week prior to deadline."*

The preference statement, like the intention statement, is powerful because of its clarity and lack of manipulation.

Putting It All Together

You can use each of these skills individually or put them together to give others a clear message of what has happened and what you would like to have happen.

For example, a dialogue with someone who has missed a critical deadline might sound like this:

> **Speak up:** *"I need to communicate something to you that is very important to me."*

> **"I" message:** *"When reports are submitted late, I get upset because it puts me in a difficult position with the committee."*

> **Intention statement:** *"My intention in telling you this is that report deadlines are crucial, and we need to talk about how deadlines can be met."*

Preference statement: *"It would be helpful to me if you could let me know if you are having difficulty with reports at least a week prior to deadline."*

This information gives people the ability to work toward problem-solving and decision-making.

When you challenge the underlying emotions of fear and anger, you are guided to greater clarity and faster resolution of problems. Bonds grow among people as they experience understanding on a psychological and emotional level.

Communication Skills for Difficult Situations

But what do you do when the situation has escalated to critical proportions? What can you do when emotions are running so high that good speaking and listening skills don't seem to be enough?

An extremely valuable communication skill when dealing with difficult situations is called *reframing*. Reframing has much in common with good listening and speaking skills, but it goes a step further to reshape information in order to explore what people care about. It is a technique that can be supportive, assertive and disarming. It reveals deeper interests—needs, fears, goals, concerns, wishes and wants.

A good time to use the reframing technique is when someone states an emphatic position such as, *"I want a raise or I quit."*

A reframing response might be: *"So it is important to you to be recognized."*

The key to this approach is to draw the focus of the conversation away from destructive criticism, blaming and manipulation through guilt. By doing this, you can explore other, more positive options for solutions.

Reframing is often difficult to use because when you hear positional statements, you tend to take them personally. You want to say: *"After all I've done for you, this is how you treat me? Well, I don't have time to listen to your complaints. Go ahead and quit if you want."*

By focusing on the interests or needs, you identify objectives for discussion. You move from endless arguing over one solution to open dialogue about options and alternatives. Reframing has similarities to paraphrasing. You are listening closely to the feeling and the facts. However, you are looking for the what, how and why of a person's intention. Therefore, reframing is a bit tricky and takes practice. When you reframe you need to:

> **1. *Capture it:*** Intuitively identify the deep need — guess what you sense you heard. Capture its essence.
>
> **2. *Cleanse it:*** Remove accusations — note what is important to the speaker, what he or she cares about and values. Clean out the negatives.
>
> **3. *Conquer it:*** Use words and actions that are responsible, affirming, inclusive and fair. Convey the sense of balance and support.
>
> **4. *Confirm it:*** Make all your words and actions positive. Confirm a forward direction.

Your needs can become confused with others' needs, if you allow your emotions to control you. You can get caught up in rescuing others so you will feel better. Reframing provides great practice in learning how to be responsible for yourself and assisting others in being responsible for themselves.

Because situations calling for reframing are often filled with emotion, it's easy to fall into negative patterns. Through persistence and focus on the positive, however, you can get the communication back on track.

Examples of Reframing

Speaker: *"What's going on? No one else gets questioned when they use their comp time."*

Reframer: *"Being treated in a way that is equal and fair is important to you."*

Speaker: *"I'm not going to be part of this project unless you are responsible for the proposal writing!"*

Reframer: *"So, sharing the workload is important to you."*

Speaker: *"This office is out of control. What a mess! I can't do anything when there are piles of paper on the desk, on the floor, everywhere."*

Reframer: *"It's important to you to have an organized place to work."*

The discussion or action that is taken after reframing depends on the conscious use of speaking and listening skills. You choose the role that you want to take in dealing with fear and anger.

To determine the role you are currently playing, ask yourself:

Do I continue the drama?

Do I strive to read other people's emotions so I can better understand their needs?

Do I want to explore this further?

Does this event really matter in the long run?

Action Guidelines

1. Learn the difference between listening and simply hearing.

2. Listen for emotion and information.

3. Determine when supportive communication would be most useful in your work environment. Determine when assertive communication would be most appropriate.

4. Practice your communication skills regularly. Experiment with different styles.

5. Allow others to have different needs and perceptions.

6. Acknowledge the importance of everyone's input in communication.

7. Think of ways to allow the other person to think and work things through.

7 TAMING THE DRAGONS IN YOUR LIFE

"I know what this is about," the dragon laughed. "You think you can control me with your sweet words!" The dragon pulled away from the brave citizen. "You silly creature! Don't you know that I'm not alone? Even if you slay me, you still have to fight all these other dragons too!" And the citizen looked around and saw that there were more dragons than she had ever imagined. More were arriving every second. As they paced back and forth, waiting to strike, she noticed that each had a silver collar. Attached to the collar that each dragon wore was a picture of the person from whom the dragon had come. She looked up at her own dragon and saw, much to her surprise, that her own picture hung on a chain around its neck. The dragon looked down at her and sneered. She shuddered and shook, not knowing quite what to do.

Emotional Problem-Solving and Decision-Making

Feelings are a significant part of every relationship. The feeling of fear, by far, destroys more relationships and lives than any other emotion.

No matter where your fears come from, one thing is certain — until you "heal the hurt," your feelings will prevent you from building positive, productive relationships with others or developing your fullest potential.

You begin to heal yourself by making a conscious decision to be receptive to change and growth in yourself and others. This receptiveness will create an environment for more successful communication, safe problem-solving and decision-making. This environment can provide a structure that encourages individual responsibility in others.

Creating the Safe Environment

In the workplace, there are many "land mines" that can blow careers to smithereens. For example, how many meetings have you attended that ended in heated arguments? How many times have you attended a meeting that seemed to serve no purpose?

It doesn't have to be that way. To make meetings more productive, you need to increase people's comfort level. When people feel comfortable and safe in expressing themselves, the possibility of effective decision-making and problem-solving grows. You can increase people's comfort level in three ways: establishing a safe atmosphere, setting the stage for agreements and applying the skills.

Establishing a Safe Atmosphere

To provide a structure that builds trust and cooperation, creates comfort, models effective interactions and empowers people, be aware of the physical environment you are working in. When you have a meeting, training session or discussion, be sure the room in which you will be conducting these activities conveys mutual respect. This may mean a round table or no table. It may mean no furniture at all. Use your best judgment for the type of environment that will make people feel the most secure.

If possible, bring color and nature into the room. Give rooms a sense of life. Let people know that they and you are connected to something greater than just doing their job.

If you are in charge of the meeting, increase the comfort level of people by making certain that there are enough chairs and tables for everyone. Have all the resources available that will be needed to conduct the meeting efficiently. Notify the appropriate persons of the meeting. Before the meeting starts, ask participants what would make them comfortable. If appropriate, arrange for refreshments. Eliminate as many distractions as possible.

When you are preparing yourself to conduct the meeting, focus on your willingness and ability to do what needs to be done for the benefit of everyone. Be sure you are thoroughly acquainted with what needs to be discussed during the meeting and the process that will be used. Trust that good results will be created in the meeting.

Setting the Stage for Agreements

The purpose of meetings should be to gather information, build relationships and agree upon desired outcomes. All too often, however, meetings have the opposite result. People are afraid to speak up. They leave the meeting feeling isolated or angry and disagreements remain unsettled. To avoid these negative results, negotiate agreements on the structure of the meetings — the *what* and *how* of the unspoken expectations of the participants.

Negotiating how you will all agree says to people, "We are cooperative and collaborative." Sometimes these initial agreements are called *ground rules*. Basic meeting agreements can be initiated by the facilitator and negotiated among the participants. Agreements that you might like to include are these suggestions adopted with permission from *Who, Me Lead A Group?* by Jean Illsley Clarke, Harper Collins © 1984:

Mutual respect

Agree to address one another with respect and listen, even if you have different ideas, approaches, opinions and perceptions.

Everyone participates

Agree that everyone will feel free to contribute his knowledge, skills, understanding and presence in the meeting. To reach the goals of the group, everyone's talents and abilities are needed.

OK to pass

Agree that everyone has the right to assimilate and integrate information in his own way. If someone needs time to think about ideas or information before expressing an opinion, the group will accept this decision.

No side conversations

Agree that individuals will avoid having side conversations. Private conversations limit involvement and interfere with the meeting's progress. Everyone needs to be fully involved in the work of the group.

Respect time

Agree to start, end and break on time. You might also ask the group to agree to take additional time to complete work assignments together.

Keep commitments

Agree to follow through on commitments. Be sure everyone understands that everyone depends on each other. When circumstances prevent someone from following through on a project or task, agree that he will give fair warning to all involved parties and renegotiate a new time line.

Decision rule

Agree on how decisions will be made. Does the group want to use majority rule, consensus or some other means?

The agreements created by a group allow everyone to understand the behavioral expectations for that group. This creates a safe atmosphere for everyone to participate and reduces fear.

In addition, create agenda items for the next meeting by questioning those in attendance. Allow everyone to have a forum for their concerns and issues. Complete the positive atmosphere by expressing appreciation for everyone's participation.

Applying the Skills

The third tool to create a safe environment is the application of skills. Communication skills, as the core of human interaction, are critical. Your communication skills determine how well you control the flow of supportive, assertive, informative and confrontational situations. You will apply your communication skills either in a group interaction or a one-on-one exchange.

A Group Interaction

Facilitating a group interaction takes a great deal of skill. If you are in charge of a meeting, it is your responsibility to make sure that everybody stays focused and clearly understands what the outcomes mean for each individual.

One-on-One Conversation

Effective communication is also essential when confronting another person who stands between you and what you think you want. The following sample dialogue is between two people.

Bob and Jackie have been working together for six months. Jackie is Bob's supervisor. She has been extremely busy with projects the last month, and Bob has found it difficult to meet with her. Bob has decided that he needs to talk with Jackie about the frustration he feels. He also wants to establish a meeting time to review a project that she delegated to him. In preparation, Bob has been practicing his communication skills. This is what happened.

Intention statement:

Bob: *"Jackie, do you have a few minutes to talk with me? I'd like to discuss something that I've been thinking about."*

Jackie: *"Bob, I'm very busy. Can't it wait?"*

Paraphrase:

Bob: *"So it's a bit much to ask for your time right now?"*

Jackie: *"Oh, I can take ten minutes. It won't kill me. We need to talk."*

Agreement statement:

Bob: *"I'm glad to hear you say that because I feel the same way. Ten minutes will do."*

Jackie: *"So, what's this about?"*

Agreement statement followed with an Intention statement:

Bob: *"There is a lot to do around here, and that's what I want to talk about. The computer programming project that you assigned to me is progressing very quickly, and I need some advice."*

Jackie: *"So, what do you need from me?"*

"I" message followed with a Preference statement:

Bob: *"When I began the project, we agreed to meet every two weeks to prevent oversights on my part and spend a lot of time correcting errors. Jackie, I become frustrated and angry when our scheduled meetings get canceled at the last minute. This has happened twice in the past month. I'd like our meetings to have top priority so I can make sure that the project is meeting your expectations."*

Jackie: *"Wait a minute, Bob. Don't make me feel guilty about those cancellations. I have had more projects dumped on me than I care to mention."*

Paraphrase:

Bob: *"So you're overwhelmed with projects."*

Jackie: *"The computer project is small potatoes compared to everything else I have going. Besides you are doing a great job, and I hate programming."*

Paraphrase:

Bob: *"Am I hearing you right? You dislike programming and you're expecting me to complete the project by myself?"*

Jackie: *"I guess that is what I'm saying."*

Intention statement followed with "I" message:

Bob: *"Jackie, I wanted to talk to you because I think we can help each other with the workload. I would feel better if my work was reviewed and there was more variety in the tasks expected of me."*

Jackie: *"What do you mean 'we can help each other,' and what other tasks are you thinking about?"*

Intention statement:

Bob: *"Well, this is the first I've heard that I'm doing great on the programming. I thought I was floundering. I'd appreciate it very much if the programming could be reviewed this week and followed by a meeting in two weeks. Then I would know if I am missing anything. Also, I would be available to take on another project, if you're willing to assign one to me."*

Jackie: *"Bob, there's no way. My schedule is jammed for the next three weeks.* (Pause) *"However, I could use your help."*

Paraphrase:

Bob: *"So it's impossible to schedule a meeting, yet I could be helpful."*

Jackie: *"Whoa! Listen to me. OK. Let's compare our schedules and find a block of time. How important is this meeting to you? Would early morning be acceptable?"*

Bob: *"Very important, and early is fine."*

Jackie: *"Bob, I could do that. But it seems that I get stuck putting in more hours than anyone else around here."*

Reframe:

Bob: *"It's really important for you to have a more manageable work life."*

Jackie: *"Yeah. And how am I supposed to do that with all these demands on me?"*

Paraphrase followed with a Preference statement:

Bob: *"You sound overwhelmed with all the work, like me with this programming project. Jackie, I am willing to help you, and I'd like your assessment of what has been done so far on the programming project."*

Jackie: *"OK. This sounds good. How does your schedule look for tomorrow morning at 7 a.m.? The sooner I review your work, the sooner I can select another project for you. I've got one in mind, and we can discuss it tomorrow. How about 45 minutes on the programming and 15 minutes on a new project?"*

Agreement statement followed with "I" message:

Bob: *"7 a.m. is a good time. Let's spend the time as you're suggesting, and I agree that we need to complete the project. By giving your attention like you just have, I'm confident that we can finish this project and work together effectively on others. Thanks for acknowledging my concerns about time and the need for review."*

Jackie: *"No problem. For our meeting tomorrow morning, can you list questions about the project that need review and indicate if you have any recommendations on how to proceed?"*

Bob: *"I sure can. Onward and upward! Thanks, Jackie."*

As Bob's example shows us, with preparation and practice, you can increase the effectiveness of your communication skills. You can also help the people you work with improve their communication skills as well.

The following exercises will help you hone your communication skills and improve decision-making and problem-solving in the workplace.

Learning to Use "I" Messages and Reframing

This exercise helps employees shift their emotional reactions to specific issues. It moves people forward into problem-solving. You can walk people through this exercise, or ask them to complete it on their own, following these steps:

1. Determine which of these emotions describes you. Complete the sentence that is most appropriate for you:

   "I am mad (angry, upset) when ..."

   "I am sad (disappointed, disheartened) when ..."

   "I am glad (happy, thrilled) when ..."

   "I am scared (afraid, petrified) when ..."

2. In light of this emotion and the circumstances that cause you to feel this way, what would you like to happen?

3. If you could come to work tomorrow and find that a miracle has happened to resolve the problem that is causing this emotion, what would be changed?

4. What do you need to have happen for this miracle to occur?

5. How would you like to see this miracle happen?

This exercise helps you identify what you care about. Once the need is identified, you can brainstorm your options. If you use it in a group, you will find that this exercise allows people to feel, determine the message their emotions are giving, clarify what is happening within themselves and visualize potential objectives.

After you have done this, practice your problem-solving skills by using paraphrasing and reflective listening techniques. Ask employees the following questions.

Step 1   **Preliminaries**

Honor time/place: *"Is this a good time to talk? Is
                                              this a good place?"*

Step 2   **Problem**

Request entry: *"I sense that you are frustrated;
                                              has something happened that
                                              upsets you?"*

(You paraphrase the answer.)

Consequences: *"What does this mean to you?"*

(Use reflective listening to
respond to the answer.)

Check emotions: *"I'm not sure I understand; how
                                              are you feeling about this?"*

(Paraphrase the answer.)

Step 3   **Potential**

Confirm past: *"Has this happened before? How
                                              was it handled?"*

(Use reflective listening to
respond to the answer.)

Clarify wishes: *"What would you like to have hap-
                                              pen?"*

(Paraphrase the answer.)

Scan potentials: *"What options are available to
                                              you?"*

(Use reflective listening to
respond to the answer.)

Step 4	**Plan**
Elicit reality:	*"What must happen? When is that going to occur?"*
(Paraphrase the answer.)	
Formulate action:	*"What is your plan?"*
(Paraphrase the answer to reinforce the plan.)	

Step 5	**Pleasantries**
Inquire about help:	*"Are you needing help? What would that be?"*
Commitment:	*"I am willing to ..."*
Appreciation:	*"You have really thought this through. Thanks for letting me know because it helps me understand your situation."*

Dealing with A.N.G.E.R. by Using Paraphrasing and Reflective Listening

When you are dealing with an angry person, it is even more important to use paraphrasing and reflective listening techniques. Hear, understand and act on the message of an angry speaker by following these essential steps.

1. Acknowledge the speaker's need for respect and be prepared by:

Knowing guidelines and procedures.

Remembering your previous contact with the person.

Knowing the details of work plans, resources and schedules.

Focusing on the speaker's experience.

Establishing positive contact and attending to comfort.

Observing body language.

2. *No interruptions:*

Provide privacy and control the environment.

Listen to understand content and acknowledge feelings.

Don't take statements personally.

3. *Genuine* statements and behavior:

Communicate fairness through your behavior and tone.

Be open about what you are doing.

State genuine and appropriate regret with a statement such as, *"It's unfortunate that happened."*

4. *Empathize* with the other person using statements such as:

"I understand that you are upset/annoyed because ..."

Don't judge, defend, excuse, rationalize or attack.

5. *Respond* by clarifying and stating positive actions you can take to resolve the problem. Check your perceptions:

"What has happened to give you the impression you were not listened to?"

"What I can do is ... Is this agreeable to you?"

Briefly summarize what has been said. Write this down on your calendar in the speaker's presence with dates that you will fulfill your commitment to him. Thank the speaker and confirm follow-up by saying:

"Thanks for helping me understand your problem. My understanding of what has happened is that ... We will meet next week on Tuesday at 9 a.m. to review what has happened. OK?"

95

Resolving Fear and Anger

It's not easy to eliminate fear and anger in the workplace. Fear and anger are often reflections of long-standing problems within the organization. A commitment to creating a safe environment and to developing effective ways to communicate is essential if you hope to succeed. Be patient and stick to your long-term goal. Don't get discouraged or think you have failed if your efforts appear to unleash a mine field of anger and fear. If that happens, you're probably on the right track. Emotions that have been buried and unsafe to air must come to the surface and be recognized before they can be dealt with. Maintain your focus on the process, and rejoice that others are beginning to feel safe enough to come forward with their fears and anger.

Action Guidelines

1. Validate emotions.

2. Ask others what makes them feel safe.

3. Use your skills to facilitate meetings.

4. Don't take reactions as personal attacks.

5. Let communication be a vehicle for understanding.

6. Experiment with your skills for decision-making and problem-solving.

8 LIVING WITH YOUR DRAGONS

The citizen thought and thought as the dragons gathered around. She thought so hard that her head started to pound. And then ... it came to her, out of the blue. She had the power. She knew what to do. "Come closer," she urged them. "Come hear what I say. Let's have a party to brighten our day!"

The Influence of Emotions

Other people's emotions can influence our own and draw us into behaviors that are ineffective, negative and counterproductive. It is important not to become overly fearful or angry in response to others' fear and anger. Managers especially need to take conscious and positive action when challenging the behaviors and choices of employees, always keeping in mind that people want to be cared for. They want to assist in creating organized methods and procedures to ensure a constructive work environment, especially if it is genuinely modeled for them and good intention is evident.

That's why it's important not to focus too much attention on angry responses or resistance. You can be highly influenced by these emotions in others through your own negative emotional responses to them. Rather than resisting or constantly confronting fear and anger, you can organize and activate the strengths and potential of your co-workers. Negativity then finds less opportunity to control how you work together.

The Role of Ethics and Ethical Behavior

Often, we have the illusion that relationships in the workplace are somehow different than in the rest of the world. This isn't true. No matter where you are, relationships are always a sacred trust. Through your relationships, you have the opportunity to be a living example of your values. Those values might include compassion, unity, truthfulness, fairness, tolerance, responsibility, respect for life and service to others. Your values are the ethical standards by which you choose to live your life.

Ethics are a set or system of values and principles of conduct. All people have their own definitions of what is important to them and how that should be presented to the greater world. The workplace needs a clear definition of ethical behavior. Managers play a crucial role in displaying behaviors that foster trust. Nevertheless, sometimes your conduct may violate your principles. You may hurt others unwittingly and fuel fear by exploding in anger over small events. When that happens, it's often an indication that you are denying your need for equilibrium in your life.

The Need for Equilibrium

Relationships are most effective when there is a state of balance or equilibrium between people. With this state of balance, a person feels safe. As a result, there is no need to seek protection, no fear of feeling forgotten or neglected. There is a willingness to give. On the other hand, a person will demand protection and require attention when she feels unsafe or if the relationship seems out of balance. Warning signals go off when you don't feel an equal exchange in a relationship. Most of the time, you expect something in return for what you have given, but it is an understanding you rarely discuss.

When this need for balance is not met, it can have far-reaching effects on the trust that is required in a good relationship. For example, two co-workers — Sally and Chris — often share office items. One day, Sally asked Chris if she could borrow some stationery. Chris gave it to her, and Sally left without saying, "Thank you." Chris didn't consciously pay any attention to her lack of courtesy because he was busy, but it registered in his subconscious.

The next day, Chris asked Sally for some paper clips. Sally gave him the clips and Chris said, "Thank you," reflecting the value he puts on courtesy to others.

A couple of days went by and Sally asked Chris if she could borrow his scissors. He gave them to her. Since Sally doesn't put a value on the conventions of courtesy, she said nothing.

Now, this scene can be played over and over with no significant problems arising. Chris might get annoyed about what he perceives as Sally's poor manners, but it's highly unlikely that he will make an event out of it.

Then one day, it erupted. Chris and Sally had to work together with a client. After a particularly important meeting, Chris became rankled about the way Sally acted around the client. He felt that her ungracious behavior was jeopardizing the project, and he told her so. Sally didn't see the problem. In her view, no problem existed. But on a deep level, Chris felt betrayed by Sally — and all because she didn't think it was important to say "thank you" when she borrowed items from him. Meanwhile, Sally became defensive. She avoided taking responsibility for her role in creating the problem by accusing Chris of being petty and getting angry with him for "trying to impose old-fashioned standards on her." Because she was afraid that Chris thought she was ill-mannered and "low rent," she defended her self-esteem by attacking him.

Accepting the Responsibility for Creating Problems

When people form relationships, they combine their thoughts, perspectives, emotions, differences and discoveries. They influence each other. Each person shares responsibility for their choices that affect the development and growth of the relationship — or its demise.

When you deny responsibility for your role in creating problems in relationships, you are dismissing the basic tenet of relationships — shared responsibility. Since relationships are dependent upon the shared reponsibility for mutual affirmation and self-worth, if one person refuses to provide that affirmation, fear and anger build, and the relationship fails. Trust is destroyed, productivity stymied.

Freedom of Choice

When you don't trust people to give you what you need in relationships, you may resort to devious ways to get them to do what you want. Control and manipulation often work so well that you become blind to the subtleties of your behavior and actions. The shock of someone doing their own thing has the effect of a wake-up call on your behavior and attitudes.

But this doesn't occur without a price. Fears of separation, being alone, abandonment, distrust and annihilation begin to haunt you. You forget that you live in a creative, unfolding world. You may be in a relationship, but you know that it is built on shaky ground. The bottom line is that *people have a right to make their own choices* and their choices may or may not include what we wish to have happen.

A one-sided perspective develops if you feel you haven't received equal to what you have given, that others are responsible for creating problems, or that others shut you out. All too often, that perspective leads you to believe that you have the right to destroy relationships. You feel entitled to end your connections with others when you cast yourself as the victim. You feel entitled to hurt others, as you feel you have been hurt. This behavior has a name — Destructive Entitlement.

How We Use Destructive Entitlement

Destructive entitlement is devastating to relationships. It builds walls that can be impossible to break down. It creates hard feelings that can last for years.

For example, Joan, a manager, had agreed to give Bryan, a well-thought-of employee, a letter of reference when he received a highly lucrative job offer. During a staff meeting, however, Joan got angry with Bryan because of some of his comments. After the meeting, Bryan went to Joan's office to pick up the letter, as they had agreed. When she invited him into her office, however, Joan stated, *"You know, Bryan, you aren't that good of an employee. You will never get a job in this line of business anyway, so I've decided not to give you a reference."*

If Joan had cooled down before talking to Bryan, she might have made a more rational decision. However, at this critical moment, she feels that Bryan has done her in, and so she wants to get even. In the process, she has destroyed the relationship.

If you feel entitled to destroy relationships, ask yourself these questions:

Is there a core issue that is bothering me that hasn't come to the surface?

Does my problem have to do with something that has never been communicated?

What deep wound has not been addressed?

Can I admit that I have been hurting someone?

What have I not been taking responsibility for in my relation-ships?

What fears have I been believing?

What is my anger really saying?

It takes conscious effort to continually operate with good intentions to turn the effects of fear and anger into good purposes. The most important of these intentions is to see the workplace as a fertile field for learning from past errors and past successes.

In your efforts, strive to eliminate coercion and manipulation from your repertoire of management techniques. Free choice is a major functioning principle. Whenever conscious coercion and manipulation are used to influence human free choice, fear and anger can only grow.

A word of caution, however: Until you have experienced drastic results from your negative behavior and suffered from harmful choices, you may not be able to see the destruction of your behavior. It is difficult — and painful — but try to get feedback about how your behavior is seen by others. Involve others in your personal growth, asking them to help you learn to be a better manager.

How to Create Unity in the Workplace

People instinctively want to be part of an organization that values them and is successful. The support that you need from others is already there, though it may not be obvious. Fear often is more manageable than it appears because co-workers want to be productive, constructive and forward thinking.

But people need leadership with integrity. They need an environment where there is spoken, conscious good intention that is motivated by concern for everyone.

It is essential to identify individual and group fears. As a manager, you need to be committed to directing others to think about ways to produce positive actions. As a manager, it is your job to look for the potential for positive growth. Your job is to strengthen and utilize the good characteristics of others.

Creating unity in the workplace should be your first concern. This goal is far more important than attempting to prevent outbursts of anger or hostility. Ironically, when you spend the majority of your energy on preventing anger from occurring, you contribute towards the creation of an unsafe atmosphere and a perception of separation. And when we feel we are all separate, it gives us justification for retaining our prejudices, for seeing others as enemies and for maintaining self-righteous independence.

The cure for this is the development of a deep sense of community — an attitude that says, "We're all in this together." You and your co-workers are a community. You all share the same needs, the same fears, the same ability to become angry. To heal hostility, encourage open communication throughout the organization. Break down the barriers and work together to solve your problems. Trust the common thread that runs through you and the people you work with. Trust that they have the same goals as you do and that they are responsible enough to work towards those goals if given the opportunity.

The Negative Impact of Linear Thinking

The work world is undergoing tremendous changes. All around us are signs that companies are learning the value of providing a safe environment for people to work in. More and more, we hear about management working toward open communication with employees. Quality circles are being formed. Self-directed teams manage projects. Enlightened companies welcome feedback from their employees and provide an environment to encourage it.

You may even be seeing some of these changes in your own company. Does this change fill you with excitement and hope? Or do you find yourself feeling even more fear and dread?

If positive changes in your workplace make you feel fearful, you may be limiting yourself with linear thinking. In linear thinking, you assume that everything is separate from everything else. You assume that one part of the system can grow while another part suffers.

An example of linear thinking would be a belief that although most of your employees are irresponsible, this does not affect production or profit. If your employees are irresponsible, it is impossible for it *not* to affect production. Profit is surely being drained from the company but you may not know it because this is the way it's always been. If you can implement changes that are needed to work more cooperatively with all employees, you will be astounded at the results.

Linear thinking may also affect your personal productivity. For example: You may decide that you are tired of all the negativity and anger in your workplace. You decide there are too many people who are angry. So you fire all of the angry folks and replace them with people who have better attitudes.

But what happens? If you don't look at the larger picture and explore the deeper causes of the problem, firing people will only increase the fear level and further erode the employees' trust of the organization. New people you hire to fill the vacant spots will quickly pick up on the fear and anger around them, and add their own to the pot!

If your management style isn't working, try a new kind of thinking. Look for whole patterns. As an exercise, see people and departments as interconnected and interdependent. Picture a flowchart of relationships, communication links and shared needs. When you try to fix a problem in one area, you might be creating problems in another area.

That's why your focus must be on the big picture. To be effective, visualize your workplace as a total system. View your work environment in terms of relationships and focus your efforts on the greatest good for the greatest number.

Nine Qualities of a Positive Relationship

This wider view is particularly important when you are building positive relationships. The following qualities are essential if you are going to have positive working relationships:

1. *Mutual Respect.* Appreciate differences. Be willing to listen and learn from others. Be willing to assist others.

2. *Open and Direct Communication.* Make a commitment to being open with others. Share your true feelings and thoughts. Encourage others to share their thoughts with you. Be worthy of the trust they show you. Trust them to have good ideas.

3. *Commitment to Shared Goals.* Identify what is important for you and your team to succeed. State your goals and ask for input. Allow others to *buy-in* to the overall plan.

4. *Honesty, Without Threat of Reprimands.* Be honest with others and encourage them to be honest with you. If there are ground rules that must be followed, negotiate them up front. Eliminate emotional reactions to the honesty of others so there will be no chance of conscious or unconscious retaliation in the future.

5. *Creative Problem-Solving.* Look at the bigger picture. Allow yourself and others to dream about a "perfect" world. Reward creativity that is focused toward solving a group problem even if it doesn't work. Encourage people to take risks.

6. *Sense of Pleasure and Joy.* Find something each day to enjoy about working with your co-workers. Let them know it's a pleasure to work with them. Celebrate achievements.

7. *Safety.* Allow people to feel that it is safe to ask for what they need. Control your emotions.

8. *Be a Sounding Board.* Let people know that you will be their "safety net" and that you expect them to be yours. Encourage everyone to view you and their co-workers as resources for their success.

9. *Acknowledge Each Other's Power.* Act on ideas, choices and decisions that have been initiated by employees. Give them credit for what they have done.

These qualities form the foundation for balanced, interdependent relationships. They open up the doors for exchange within a relationship and allow everyone to work together for a common good. Adopt these guidelines as shared expectations and use them to build a framework for behavior in the workplace.

Developing Trust

One of the unwritten messages that people are constantly sending is this: "I want to trust the people around me." Nevertheless, people operate from their contradictory beliefs: They do not trust that others will keep their commitments. They do not trust that they themselves will keep commitments. They do not trust themselves.

It is sometimes difficult to trust others or ourselves. One of the primary fears of all people is commitment. Therefore, you may do things that undermine your own true inner beliefs, i.e., you may say, "I am trustworthy," but act on beliefs and assumptions developed by past negative, shaming experiences. In short, you don't feel good about yourself.

It is hard to build relationships without fear if those negative beliefs and assumptions rule. But it can be done, and it is done by *redefining those beliefs and assumptions.*

Learning the Concept of Acceptance

Trying to break through negative patterns of communication is futile if people do not allow others to change, do not accept that everyone participates in her own personal development, do not accept that everyone needs to assist in each other's development or do not accept differences.

Some people never seem to change, no matter what you do or how hard you try. Finally, you throw up your hands and say, "He'll never change." But take a moment and think about the logic of that assumption. Are you the same person you were 20 years ago? Are you the same person you were 20 minutes ago? Your life can change in an instant. So can the lives of others.

You are constantly changing. Most of the time you are unaware of this change until an event brings it to your attention. You may not like change. You may even deny that change happens in your life. You may try to trick yourself into thinking life is what you experience. In truth, however, your life is what you create.

A cardinal rule of relationships is this: Each individual is evolving.

Inner personal growth is a creative process. The process for that evolution differs with each person. You can't control change in other people. You can't force them to grow. You can only provide the opportunity and the environment for the seeds of positive change to take root.

If you decide that nothing can be done to improve a relationship, then you must accept the other person as he is. You must respect his personal growth rate and nurture him through basic concepts that keep the door open for growth. These concepts are called Universal Practices.

Implementing Universal Practices in Working Relationships

Universal practices are things you can do to foster honesty, safety and integrity in all people.

Universal practices heal you and others. They allow you to take control of the way you act and think, and you can change how you relate to others, no matter how they relate to you.

Universal Practice 1: Believe in yourself — Believe that you have the resources and knowledge to respond to emotional situations. You are responsible for bringing your best forward and you can learn from each interaction. Trust yourself to bring attitudes and behaviors into the workplace that build positive relationships.

Universal Practice 2: Cooperate — Model a winning attitude. Empower others to solve problems, make decisions and do their jobs. Find ways to meet other people's needs and resolve common concerns. A cooperative attitude is contagious and everyone benefits!

Universal Practice 3: Keep agreements — When you agree to do something, do it. Make your agreements your top priority. Allow others to depend on you to keep your commitments or renegotiate if circumstances have affected your ability to follow through.

Universal Practice 4: Tell the truth — Tell yourself the truth about interactions and situations, then speak up for yourself. Stop yourself if you want to speak out of imagined fears or if your intention is to hurt another person.

Universal Practice 5: Give and get feedback — Check your assumptions and clarify your perceptions by asking others to give you their interpretations of your conversations, behaviors and performance. Ask others if they are interested in receiving feedback — not criticism — about their work.

Universal Practice 6: Respect life — Be sensitive to the lessons you learn from others.

Universal Practice 7: Offer forgiveness — Forgiveness allows you to release resentment and give others permission to change. As the forgiver, you are free from the past and able to act in the present.

It's not a perfect world. Fear and anger are very real. Only *you* can overcome the fear and anger in your world. Only *you* can trust others and allow them to trust you. Only you can tame your dragons of fear and anger and become the master of yourself.

Action Guidelines

1. See the potential in co-workers.

2. Allow others to ask for what they need.

3. Take responsibility for using your power, making choices and encouraging growth in relationships.

4. Allow others to think for themselves and make their own choices.

5. Transform fear into positive action.

6. Develop a sense of community.

7. See co-workers as interdependent and interconnected.

8. Commit to shared goals.

9. Follow the universal practices.

Epilogue:

So the citizen and the dragons sat down to talk. They talked and they talked. They cried some too. They looked at their anger and they looked at their fear, and then they had tea cakes while they looked in a mirror. And when they saw what was reflected, there was a miraculous feat. The dragons started shrinking and dozed off to sleep. When the citizen saw what happened, she couldn't help but smile. She whispered, "Sleep well, gentle dragons. I'll see you in a while."

Conclusion

Everybody experiences fear and anger at times in their lives, but nobody wants to talk about it. Fear and anger are "dark" emotions. And when these emotions are unleashed, they seem to control our minds, our bodies, our entire outlook on life. When we are in the grip of fear and anger, we will gladly destroy relationships and turn down opportunities.

Fear and anger are especially prevalent in the workplace. As a manager, your task is not only to take charge of your own fear and anger, but to help others manage their dark emotions too. If fear and anger in your workplace is not addressed, it grows, spreading like a cancer, stripping people of their incentive, robbing the company of potential profits, thwarting your dreams and ambitions.

There are no quick fixes or easy answers for the "best" way to handle fear and anger. There is only one essential maxim: You have to allow yourself to feel your emotions. You have to allow the dragons of fear and anger to come out of their dark caves and into the light of knowledge so you can do battle with them — and learn to control them.

The handling of fear and anger in the workplace begins with you. As a manager, you are responsible and accountable for your actions. You can't afford to allow fear and anger to block the potential that is within you and cloud the issues when you are making decisions and solving problems. You can't afford to allow the people you work with to waste their talents and do less than their best because fear and anger command more attention than their work.

Use this handbook to continue to stimulate your thoughts about fear and anger. Argue with the definitions and examples. Write in the margins. Create your own understanding of your situation. Develop dialogues that will help you manage the fear and anger in your workplace, and slay those dragons.

INDEX

Buy any 3, get 1 FREE!

Get a 60-Minute Training Series™ Handbook FREE ($14.95 value)*
when you buy any three. See back of order form for full selection of titles.

These are helpful how-to books for you, your employees and co-workers. Add to
your library. Use for new-employee training, brown-bag seminars, promotion gifts and
more. Choose from many popular titles on a variety of lifestyle, communication, productivity
and leadership topics. Exclusively from National Press Publications.

DESKTOP HANDBOOK ORDER FORM

Ordering is easy:

1. Complete both sides of this Order Form, detach, and mail, fax or phone your order to:

      Mail: National Press Publications
                 P.O. Box 419107
                 Kansas City, MO 64141-6107

   Fax: 1-913-432-0824
   Phone: 1-800-258-7248
   Internet: http://www.natsem.com

2. Please print:

Name_____ Position/Title _____

Company/Organization_____

Address_____City _____

State/Province_____ZIP/Postal Code _____

Telephone (____)_____ Fax (____)_____

3. Easy payment:

❑ Enclosed is my check or money order for $_____ (total from back).
   Please make payable to National Press Publications.

Please charge to:
❑ MasterCard   ❑ VISA   ❑ American Express

Credit Card No. _____ Exp. Date_____

Signature_____

• •

MORE WAYS TO SAVE:

SAVE 33%!!! BUY 20-50 COPIES of any title ... pay just $9.95 each ($11.25 Canadian).

SAVE 40%!!! BUY 51 COPIES OR MORE of any title ... pay just $8.95 each ($10.25 Canadian).

* $17.00 in Canada

Buy 3, get 1 FREE!

60-MINUTE TRAINING SERIES™ HANDBOOKS

TITLE	RETAIL PRICE	QTY	TOTAL
8 Steps for Highly Effective Negotiations #424	$14.95		
Assertiveness #4422	$14.95		
Balancing Career and Family #415	$14.95		
Delegate for Results #4592	$14.95		
The Essentials of Business Writing #4310	$14.95		
Exceptional Customer Service #4882	$14.95		
Fear & Anger: Slay the Dragons… #4302	$14.95		
Fundamentals of Planning #4301	$14.95		
Getting Things Done #4112	$14.95		
How to Coach an Effective Team #4308	$14.95		
How to De-Junk Your Life #4306	$14.95		
How to Handle Conflict and Confrontation #4952	$14.95		
How to Manage Your Boss #493	$14.95		
How to Supervise People #4102	$14.95		
How to Work With People #4032	$14.95		
Inspire & Motivate: Performance Reviews #4232	$14.95		
Listen Up: Hear What's Really Being Said #4172	$14.95		
Motivation and Goal-Setting #4962	$14.95		
A New Attitude #4432	$14.95		
The New Dynamic Comm. Skills for Women #4309	$14.95		
Parenting: Ward & June… #486	$14.95		
The Polished Professional #4262	$14.95		
The Power of Innovative Thinking #428	$14.95		
The Power of Self-Managed Teams #4222	$14.95		
Powerful Communication Skills #4132	$14.95		
Present With Confidence #4612	$14.95		
The Secret to Developing Peak Performers #4692	$14.95		
Self-Esteem: The Power to Be Your Best #4642	$14.95		
Shortcuts to Organized Files & Records #4307	$14.95		
The Stress Management Handbook #4842	$14.95		
Supreme Teams: How to Make Teams Work #4303	$14.95		
Thriving on Change #4212	$14.95		
Women and Leadership #4632	$14.95		

Sales Tax
All purchases subject to state and local sales tax.
Questions?
Call
1-800-258-7248

Subtotal	$
Add 7% Sales Tax *(Or add appropriate state and local tax)*	$
Shipping and Handling *($3 one item; 50¢ each additional item)*	$
TOTAL	$